C000224657

80003358920

A Brief History
of Whistling

Why no whistlers?

SIR—Until comparatively recently, one often heard men as they wended their way to work whistling merrily. Errand boys also whistled and so did many postmen.

Although the whistling may not have been very musical, it was always possible to recognise the tune.

Now I never hear anyone whistling in the street. Why?

GORDON H. LUCK
Hassocks, Sussex.

Daily Telegraph 7th January 1978

A Brief History of Whistling

John Lucas and
Allan Chatburn

Five Leaves Publications

www.fiveleaves.co.uk

A Brief History of Whistling
by John Lucas and Allan Chatburn

Published in 2013
by Five Leaves Publications,
PO Box 8786,
Nottingham NG1 9AW
www.fiveleaves.co.uk

Copyright © John Lucas and Allan Chatburn, 2013

Every effort has been made to contact the copyright holders
of illustrations and photographs. We would be pleased to hear from
further copyright holders so we can give due credit in subsequent editions.

ISBN: 978-1-907869 - 88-4

Designed and typeset by
Four Sheets Design and Print

Cover design by Darius Hinks

Printed by Imprint Digital of Exeter

Northamptonshire Libraries & Information Service KF	
Askews & Holts	

Contents

Acknowledgements   6

Prefatory Note   7

Introduction   9

The Mechanics of Whistling   19

Whistle While You Work   33

Whistling as Self-Expression   55

Whistling as Communication   85

Whistling as Protest and Resistance   116

Whistling as Entertainment   132

Acknowledgements

The authors wish to acknowledge helpful suggestions and information provided by the following: Julie Astill, Al Atkinson, Ross Bradshaw, Derrick Buttress, Dr. Swee-Hoon Chouh, Joy Dee, Michael Eaton, the late Mervyn Gould, Dr. Basil Haynes, Sarah Hoskiss, London Sound Survey, Amanda and Macayla Riney-Lucas, Paul McLoughlin, Joseph Pridmore, Maurice Rutherford, J.M. Schlitz, Jenny Swann, Peter Vacher, Dr. Sam Ward, John Hartley Williams.

Especial thanks are due to Sheila Harrod, World Whistling Champion, for sharing with us her knowledge of the life of a professional whistler and for allowing us access to the papers of Cloudsley Seddon, who, before his death in 1975, had begun preparing his own History of Whistling. And many thanks to Stephen Neeston for demonstrating the whistling instructions required by a shepherd working with a dog.

Prefatory Note

The following book makes no attempt at a prescriptive definition of the nature of whistling. Although our main concern is with human whistling, we take account of mechanical whistles as well as pipes, flutes, and penny whistles. We also have much to say about the whistling of birds, especially that which interacts with human whistling. But because we aren't trying to write a definitive history of whistling our book is by no means as copiously illustrative as would be possible. Any reader of what follows will be able to think of examples of melodies which we could have cited as at one time or another popular in whistled form, on the streets or in other public places, especially buses and trains. Moreover, because whistled sounds can often seem ambiguous, many of the examples we give may well seem arbitrarily allotted to certain chapters. Why here? Why not there? But this is the nature of whistling. It can be as ironically intended as it is seemingly innocent; it can communicate while being self-expressive; it can be both protest and delight. To quote the words of Edward Thomas in his poem "The Penny Whistle," a whistled tune may well be "saying more" than words can. In the hope of avoiding undue repetition, though some is inevitable, we have therefore decided to give examples of whistling wherever they figure as useful illustrations of our narrative, while being only too aware that they could as justifiably occur at a different place in the stories we have to tell.

J.L. and A.C.

Introduction

Old houses were scaffolding once
and workmen whistling

T.E. Hulme's "Image" was written just before WW1. It therefore belongs to the period during which "Robert Tressell" (the pseudonym of Robert Noonan, 1870-1911) wrote, though he did not find a publisher for, *The Ragged-Trousered Philanthropists*.

Not much cause for whistling there, you might think. The workers about whom Tressell writes — painters, decorators, and plasterers — were banned from both singing and whistling. And yet whistling and work go together. Whistling is an expression of jaunty defiance, of independence of mind if not body. You could even think of it as the working man's *metier*. After all, according to the Oxford English Dictionary, *metier* is:

1. A profession or trade, esp. that to which one is well suited.
2. A person's strong point or speciality.

Whistling is the token of independent labour. The shepherd on the hillside, the tinker in the lonely lane, the craftsman — woodcarver, blacksmith, weaver — plying his skill in the workshop. Each is in his element, so the cliché goes. And an expressive part of that element is whistling. Hence, the workmen on their scaffolding. Hence, R.S. Thomas's report of Hugh Puw. "What shall I say?/I have heard him whistling in the hedges/On and on."

Whistling seems to be general, universally practised even, among those whose labour, whether skilled or unskilled, whether pursued

9

under a roof or in the open air, identifies them as working-class, artisanal, peasant-like. And it isn't restricted to working-class experience. "Everybody whistles," says the protagonist of Kafka's last short story, "Josefine, the Singer, or the Mouse People," a story about which there will be more to say in the final chapter of this book. Nevertheless, it's probably safe to assert that street whistling, as well as whistling more generally in the open air, belongs with those who are most used to working in the open. Errand boys on their bikes whistled. Postmen afoot or on horseback whistled. So did ploughmen, carters, bargees ... the list goes on. There's not much point in trying to enumerate the whistlers. It's enough to say that in Western culture whistling was common practice, the practice of the commonalty. Nor was it consequent on or coincidental with the coming of industrialisation. Goatherds in ancient Ilyria whistled, so, no doubt, did the crewmen of Jason's Argo. And we have it on Homer's authority that during a night raid among the Trojan forces, Odysseus and Diomed communicated with each other by whistling.

But at this point a distinction needs to be made. Hulme's workmen whistling on their scaffolding are making music. Their whistling, while perhaps a token of independent spirit, is assuredly recreational. Whistle while you work. Whistling in this sense is the ultimate do-it-yourself music, the most democratic art. But the Ilyrian goatherd was sending out instructions, calling his goats to attend. His whistling is therefore functional, intrinsic to the work being done. Whistling in this sense is communication. The men on the scaffolding could, after all, get by without whistling. The goatherd couldn't. Nor could the shepherd whistling to his dog. Nor could a mariner who whistles to a mate aloft in order to tell him to reef a sail or let one out. And although the tinker who whistles as he walks the roads may be merry, his whistling is also a sign that he's on his way. So bring out your pots and pans. This is not whistling while you work but whistling *because* you work.

And, sometimes, don't whistle. Miners were forbidden from whistling at the coal-face. Canaries were sent down pit shafts

10

because the only thing that would stop a canary from singing was methane gas. A whistling miner stopping short might, for all his mates knew, have encountered and inhaled a pocket of such gas. You could whistle at the pit head, you could whistle if you were at the bottom of the shaft and needed to attract a pit pony to come to you. That apart, no whistling.

And no whistling for theatre stage-hands. Members of the back-stage crew — the term is instructive — were often recruited from sailors on shore leave and eager to earn some money before they signed up for another voyage. Sailors knew how to handle ropes. That was why they made good stage-hands. But they were also used to obeying commands made by a piped whistle. Mouth whistling, by contrast, was thought to encourage a storm. Sailors might "whistle up the wind" when their ships were becalmed, but on the whole whistling at sea was thought to bring bad luck. Consider the old fisherman's rhyme:

> A pleasant breeze on a fine moonlight night,
> Then I began to whistle in delight!
> The mate he heard and soon called out to me,
> "You must not whistle when you are at sea."

Or consider Walter Scott's "How whistle rash bids tempests roar." (In his poem "Rokeby".) Whistle too loudly and you might bring on disaster:

> Only an hour ago
> I was whistling to St. Antonio
> For a capful of wind to fill our sail
> And instead of a breeze he sent a gale.

These lines come from Longfellow's "Golden Legend". In an early poem, "Who whistled for the wind, that it should break", Philip Larkin identifies death as emanating from "all winds crying" where

"Black flowers burst out wherever the night has dwelt." The winds whistle up death.

This may be superstition but in theatre land, especially, it has behind it a measure of good sense. Whistle back stage at the wrong moment and a fly curtain or a flat might suddenly and with catastrophic inappropriateness descend on stage, as, according to legend, happened once in pantomime at Bury St Edmunds, when an affecting hearth-side scene between Cinderella and Buttons was transformed into a busy London street which left Buttons talking to himself, Cinderella having been cut off from his presence by the descent of a fly on which was painted a parade of shops. Someone had whistled.

There was also an old belief that no Christian traveller should whistle in the dark, "else Devils will go along with him." Then again, whistling could apparently distract you from the work on which you were meant to be concentrating. "Don't whistle your work away," the fourteen-year old Derrick Buttress was told when he took up his first employment in the rag trade, in Nottingham's Lace Market. The work mostly involved stirring pots of glue used to gum up the side of cardboard boxes, hardly demanding labour. Derrick's whistling was probably seen as disrespectful of his employers, even a kind of impudence. Not dumb insolence but endlessly and in its way eloquently expressive: of incredulity, derision, contempt.

Work is common to nearly all societies. So is making music. Work and singing have always belonged together. There are, though, exceptions. In his essay "An Amateur Spy in Arabia," published in *Granta* 75, in which he recalls experiences of the late 1930s, Norman Lewis reports that in the Yemen "It was illegal to sing, and even more to whistle." Nevertheless, the generalisation stands. Work and music go together. Song may be collective utterance, as in sea shanties, the work-songs of chain-gangs, or "the singing masons building roofs of gold," as the Archbishop of Canturbury wonderfully anthropomorphises the labour of worker bees in *Henry*

V, his words summoning up not merely the building of a hive but of, say, Whitehall or the Doge's Palace. But song, like whistling, can equally well go with isolated labour such as the Solitary Reaper's, who "cuts and binds the grain/And sings a melancholy strain." *Her* song affirms human presence in and even perhaps against blank nature. "Oh, listen, for the vale profound/Is overflowing with the sound." As for the ploughboy, is it his "shrill notes," Wordsworth asks rhetorically, which "Impart new gladness to the morning air?"

Whistling is less immediately or obviously eloquent than song — though it is often interspersed with words in shanties and work songs — but while it must make do without words it can be equally subtle, perhaps more so. And of course you can whistle a song to which everyone knows the words and therefore understands your meaning. You don't have to *sing* "Kiss Me Goodnight, Sergeant-Major" to let a barrack-room in on the joke. Not singing the words is part of the joke, a way of showing your contempt for a superior officer while uttering nothing offensive. You're simply whistling a tune. But then again, whistling can redeem a fine melody from the crass words that sometimes accompany it. It concentrates attention on the melodic line. And accomplished whistlers, whether using lips alone or with fingers in the mouth, can provide trills, glissandos and vibrato, which, depending on your taste, adorn or over-enrich the tune itself. Some whistlers can even hum as they whistle.

As with song, so whistling can be collective, an expression of togetherness. Think of the famous opening of David Lean's film, *Bridge On the River Kwai:* captured British soldiers march into a Japanese war camp, whistling as they do so that jauntiest of marches, "Colonel Bogey." But whistling can be "lonesome" music. Although seldom melancholic — the commonest epithet for whistling is "jaunty" — there is no doubt that whistling heard along an empty, wet street at night, makes the emptiness even more extreme, is an almost definitive sound of melancholy isolation. The same goes for the cowboy riding his horse across the prairie. This is of course endlessly open to parody.

Similarly, jauntiness can be used to parodic ends. Not with the soldiers who whistle "Colonel Bogey," perhaps, but the whistled refrain to "Always Look on the Bright Side of Life" at the end of the Monty Python classic *Life of Brian* is a wonderful, blackly comic, spoof of cheerfulness.

Whistling is, or can be, quite remarkably subtle. It can also be remarkably eloquent and, in the words of Edward Thomas quoted later in this book, it may "say more than I am saying." Nevertheless, it used to be frowned on by those keen to stress their middle-class credentials.[1] "Whistling is the sign of a vacant mind" one of the authors of this book was told as a small boy by a neighbour when he passed her house one day, whistling. What she *really* meant was that whistling was for the working class.[2] A whistling resident threatened property values. Whistling was street music or music of the factory or building site or hillside or farm. You wouldn't hear whistling in drawing rooms or restaurants. Music halls, yes, and of these there will be much more to say in a later chapter. But then music halls were a form of working-class entertainment.

So, the streets were full of whistlers. Butchers' boys, grocers' lads, Telegram Sams, newspaper deliverers, milkmen, coal-delivery men, draymen, bus conductors .... But not women. *Never* women. "When a woman whistles the devil rattles his chains, " according to an old folk saying. and a well-known and still repeated rhyme served as a mnemonic to warn against such behaviour. In one of its several versions, it runs "Whistling women and cocksure men, Will never come to any good end." Another version has it that "A whistling woman and a crowing hen/Fetches t'owd lad [the Devil] out of his den."

There seem to have been two reasons why women should not whistle, especially in public, why it was as *infra dig* as smoking in the streets. This is a matter we take up in more detail later in the book, but here it seems appropriate to remark that one reason for the disapproval of women's whistling was that it was thought to be tarty. Prostitutes whistled for custom. Moreover, distorting the lips — puckering them — in order to whistle, took away from the perfect labiality women needed in order to attract marriage proposals. Of the two, the risk of being thought "cheap" seems to have operated as the more persuasive objection against whistling women. "When we were girls our father told my sister and me we must *never* whistle outside the house," one old lady recalled, "only 'rough' girls whistled." And she came from working-class Newcastle.

For some, a woman whistling inside the house was equally reprehensible, not to say downright dangerous. There were — there still are — communities where such whistling is said to summon up evil spirits. One version of the old belief in the Seven Whistlers was that they were the souls of Jews who had sacrificed Christ. Whistle and you risked further disaster. The Seven Whistlers might come for you.

None of these interdicts applied to men, or, for that matter, boys. The streets were full of whistlers. But not now. In a letter to the *Daily Telegraph* (where else) dated 7th January, 1978, Gordon H. Luck

15

writes that "until comparatively recently, one often heard men as they wended their way to work whistling merrily. Errand boys also whistled and so did postmen.... Now I never hear anyone whistling in the streets. Why?" Good question. Whistling may not be a lost art but it isn't any longer an omnipresence, isn't an expression of vox pop.

It was when the two of us were engaged in what we thought was casual conversation on this matter that we suddenly realised that trying to account for the comparative dearth of whistling nowadays would take us deep into aspects of popular culture and social history that, to the best of our knowledge, have not been previously written about. To put it as succinctly as possible. *Why* has whistling so declined? Is it because of the coming of the transistor and its successors, to say nothing of mobile phones and iPods? Well, possibly. Because errand boys are no more? Yes, undoubtedly. Because there are no longer any night-shift miners who, in past years, would fill the top deck of a bus and join in whistling whatever tune one of them began? Again, yes. Because social attitudes have changed? Very likely. In 2010 the American writer, Michael Chabon, wrote an affectionate piece in *The Guardian* about his father-in-law. "I didn't play golf," Chabon begins, "and he had never smoked marijuana." In addition, whereas he himself was "dubious of the motives of other people," his father-in-law was "big and placid, uniformly kind to strangers and friends, and never went anywhere without whistling a little song." There's an undeniable nostalgia about this glimpse of an earlier, less troubled, less neurotic generation, one whose easy living is expressed through or emblematised by whistled song, but on the other hand it does seem to be the case that fewer people now whistle within as well as out-of-doors than their forebears did.[3]

And yet whistling has not disappeared. Shepherds, some of them anyway, still whistle instructions to their dogs. (Others use quad bikes to round up their flocks.) You can hear the whistling of tunes, still, in the streets, it's to be found on some film soundtracks, and it's much favoured by certain folk groups. It has a *cachet* as the mark of freedom, of resistance to the tame, the conventional, the bourgeois. In this sense it can endorse a nostalgic yearning for greenwoods and the rolling road. Shedding nostalgia, it's a city sound: loud, tuneless, derisive, rising shrilly from football terraces or as the sound of protest on marches.

According to an article in the *Daily Mail* for January, 29th, 2013, whistling is used by Vietnamese mothers as a help in potty training, though the *Mail* is quick to warn its readers that the findings of a research team into the practice leave unclear "whether culture and tradition have a part to play." Moreover, "the whistling technique requires keeping babies partially or fully naked, which isn't always suitable in the British climate." No, indeed.

The following pages are in no sense meant to provide an exhaustive account of whistling. But we hope that they offer an entertaining as well as instructive history of what, for all its diminution in appeal, is almost certainly still the most widely-spread and enduring expression of popular culture.

Notes

[1] Robert Tressell was the pseudonym of Robert Noonan (1870-1911), a working-class writer who died of tuberculosis in a Liverpool workhouse, his novel still unpublished. An abridged edition of *The Ragged Trousered Philanthropists* appeared in 1914, but the first reliable edition was not published until 1955.

[2] As the present book was going to press we heard of how whistling can still incur displeasure. A milkroundsman in Leicester has been reprimanded by his employers for disturbing the sleep of residents on his round. The problem is not, so the offended parties say, the clatter of the milk cart, but the man's whistling. Admittedly, the milkman begins his round at 4.30 a.m. each morning, but his whistling, while loud — a snatch was recorded for BBC Radio 4's PM Programme on 13th July 2013 — is by no means unmelodious. One of his older customers has apparently congratulated him on it. It cheers her up. "I'm a cheerful chap," he told the BBC reporter. "I've got a job, I've been doing it for forty years, and I like whistling." But his employers, having received a number of complaints, are unrepentant about ordering him to refrain from whistling

17

until a later hour. If he doesn't do their bidding, they say, they will have no alternative but to dismiss him.

3 The father of George and Ira Gershwin, growing up poor, was an expert whistler, as were his sons. So was Louis Armstrong and so were any number of the first and second-generation of jazz musicians. It is tempting to claim that, lacking instruments, these people were nevertheless determined to make music, but it may be better to remark that as whistling is free, so satisfying the urge to "maken melodie" comes untrammelled to anyone who learns to whistle.

The Mechanics
of Whistling

I

This book is an enquiry into the history of whistling. It is therefore about why an activity once so common, so taken for granted, seems, if not by any means defunct, far less widespread among people of all ages, irrespective of class or gender. But before we begin to trace the history of whistling it seems proper to offer an explanation of what whistling actually *is*. Specialised forms of whistling — the wolf whistle, whistling to sheep dogs, whistling as a means of expressive communication between people some distance apart, for example — will be considered at the appropriate moment. So will what might be called artificial forms of whistle: the pipe, tin flute, shepherd's aid, whistles used by sports officials, and by policemen. Here, the concern is with what might be called common, garden, or street whistling, the kind of whistling to which we have given the name "mouth whistling." . How is it done?

At first glance the answer seems obvious. Simply do as is apparently innocently suggested in the Humphrey Bogart, Lauren Bacall film of *To Have and to Have Not,* "You know how to whistle, don't you, Steve? You just put your lips together and blow." As "Hamlet's aunt" remarks of "Blood" in *David Copperfield,* "We see Blood in a nose, and we know it. We meet with it in a chin, and we say "There it is! That's Blood! It is an actual matter of fact. We point it out. It admits of no doubt." We hear whistling on the streets, and we know it. It admits of no doubt. But the *definition* of whistling, at all events in Dictionary terms, does admit of doubt. To see why, we

Lauren Bacall in *To Have and to Have Not*

need do no more than consider what Samuel Johnson has to say about it in his *Dictionary of the English Language*.

Johnson is surprisingly generous in the amount of space he gives to defining an activity he might have been supposed to dislike, even despise. Whistling wasn't gentlemanly. It was at one time banned from Eton and other public schools. Given Johnson's decision to exclude from his Dictionary what in his preface he called the "terms of art and manufacture" on the grounds that he could not be expected to "visit the caverns to learn the miners' language, nor take a voyage to perfect my skills in the art of navigation, nor visit the warehouses of merchants, and shops of artificers," and in view of his refusal to take note of the "cant" terms of the "laborious and mercantile part of the people," because such language is "in a great measure casual and mutable," it seems odd that he chooses to recognise the word whistling at all, especially as he identifies the activity with such people. But whistling is spared Johnson's ultimate act of censure — exclusion — and he even cites a number of humorous examples of its use among writers he esteems. This no doubt explains why he devotes several column inches to whistling. What is good enough for Shakespeare has to be good enough for Johnson.

He begins with an attempt to describe as simply as he can how whistling is performed. This, while it is certainly a great deal more helpful than his famous definition of a net — "a texture woven with large interstices or meshes" — isn't trouble-free. First, whistle as verb.

TO WHISTLE:

1. "To form a kind of musical sound by an inarticulate modulation of the breath." [To bolster this definition, Johnson provides the following instances, beginning with two quotations from Shakespeare.] "I've watched and travell'd hard:/Some time I shall sleep out, the rest I'll *whistle.*" "His big, manly voice,/Changing again toward childish treble pipes,/He *whistles* in his sound." Then comes Milton. "While the plowman near at hand/*Whistles* o'er the furrow'd land." John Gay is also instanced: "The ploughman leaves the talk of day,/And trudging homeward *whistles* on the way." (All the emphases are Johnson's.)

Johnson then moves on to further definitions.

2. To make a sound with a small wind instrument.

3 To sound shrill. Here, Pope's version of the *Odyssey* is quoted. "The wild winds *whistle,* and the billows roar,/The splitting raft the furious tempest tore." Joseph Addison is then adduced to provide the example of whistling as a form of communication: "He chanced to miss his dog; we stood still 'till he had *whistled* him up."

Now whistle as noun.

1. Sound made by modulation of breath in the mouth.

2. A sound made by a small wind instrument.

3. The mouth: the organ of whistling.
4. A small wind instrument. Here, Johnson quotes "Behold,/Upon the hempen tackle ship boys climbing,/Hear the shrill *whistle*, which doth order give/To sounds confused."
5. The noise of winds.
6. A call, such as sportsmen use to their dogs. "Madam, here comes my lord./I have been worth the *whistle*."

For what it's worth, we should note that these last words are spoken by Goneril in *King Lear*, and according to Kenneth Muir in his Arden edition of the play, Goneril is drawing on the proverb "It's a poor dog that is not worth the whistle — or whistling." Johnson doesn't note this, nor does he remark the use of "whistle off," which is apparently a term used in falconry when the falconer allows a half-tamed bird to have its freedom. But this explains Othello's "If I do prove her haggard,/Though that her jesses were my dear heart-strings,/I'd whistle her off and let her down the wind/To prey at fortune." (A "haggard" is a half-trained hawk that has gone wild.)

Whether in this instance whistling is made by "a small wind instrument" or the falconer's own "organ of whistling" isn't clear. Of more interest, though, is that Johnson takes no note of how whistling depends not merely on the mouth, but also on the shaping and variant pressure of the lips. Perhaps he was misled or seduced by his citation from Walton's *Compleat Angler:* "Let's drink the other cup to wet our *whistles*, and so sing away all sad thoughts." Here, though wetting the lips undoubtedly helps with whistling — it's habitual to run your lips across both upper and bottom lip before beginning to whistle, and whistling with chapped lips is difficult — the word "whistle" acts as a synecdoche for the vocal organs, specifically throat and mouth.

There is, though, a more mechanical connection between drinking and whistling. In his *Dictionary of Slang and Unconventional English*, Eric Partridge includes reference to a "whistlecup," which he defines as "A drinking-cup fitted with a whistle, the last toper capable of using it receiving it as a prize: public-house coll.: from ca 1880. Also, a cup that, on becoming empty, warns the tapster." Such whistle cups were certainly around before the last years of the 19th century. One is mentioned in *The Pickwick Papers*, and still earlier it became the habit to summon tapsters for a refill by whistling for their attention.

The O.E.D. doesn't mention whistlecups. It does, though, provide a clearer definition than Johnson of what whistling entails. "An act of whistling: a clear shrill sound produced by forcing the breath through the narrow opening made by contracting the lips (and sometimes by inserting two fingers) used esp. as a call or signal or to express surprise, approval, or derision ...." But can these very different sounds be made the same way? A whistle of surprise is often — usually? — made by sucking-in air through not so much pursed as taut lips. That's very different from the blowing out through rounded lips required for loud whistles of derision. Whistled approval is always, surely, made by the forced exhalation of breath through lips that are pursed? Though Johnson does not distinguish between these sounds, he would undoubtedly call them all "inarticulate" because for him "articulate" means "sounds varied and changing at proper pauses, in opposition to the voices of animals, which admit no such variety." Moreover, "an *articulate* pronunciation" is "a manner of speaking clear and distinct, in which one sound is not confounded with another."

We leave until later in this book instances of villages which communicate with one another by whistling and whistling alone, together with an explanation of the complex techniques required to put into operation this whistled "speech," although acquiring and then mastering these undoubtedly takes a good deal of practice. They certainly can't be achieved by simply putting your lips together and blowing. We also leave until the appropriate moment a discussion of the kind of whistling common among professional entertainers, who use two, three, or even four fingers in the mouth to produce sounds which are remarkable for volume — this is some-times aided by the use of the free hand as a kind of tympan, with palm loosely cupped above the fingers of the other hand — as well as for range and expressiveness, including wide vibrato, glissando, and, among the most skilful, the effect of treble-tonguing common to cornet and trumpet players, and which is astonishingly accurate in pitch when managed with musical accompaniment. Here, it is enough to note that Johnson accepts that a Whistler is one who whistles, and that this implies, even takes for granted, severe limits of articulacy. He quotes Addison: "The prize was a guinea to be conferr'd upon the ablest whistler, who could whistle clearest, and go through his tune without laughing." But he has nothing to say about the musical articulation of bird song. Nor does he believe that whistling can carry wide varieties of meanings. Or if he does, he keeps quiet about it.

One purpose of whistling is to send signals. Johnson acknowl-edges the piping that tells ships' boys what to do with "hempen tackles," but for perhaps understandable reasons he thinks the ploughman's whistling is purely recreational rather than, as it more usually is, an instruction to his team of horses or a means to keep them at it. As cows which are given names are said to produce more milk, so plough-horses worked more steadfastly to the accompani-ment of the ploughman's whistle. Johnson would have been unlikely to know of this. And, unsurprisingly, he has nothing to say of the manner in which shepherds whistle instructions to the dogs who guard and guide their flocks. Johnson was a townsman. There were things he could afford — or effect — not to know.

But it does come as a surprise to find that he should make no mention of that highly articulate form of whistling, the secret, coded language which criminals use in order to communicate with each other. Knowledge of such language explains why, at the upper end of Piccadilly's Burlington Arcade, the one that opens onto Cork Street, a brass plate screwed to the wall stipulates the right of Beadles to eject anyone from the Arcade who is deemed to be behaving in an unseemly manner. In practice, this tended to mean anyone caught whistling, not so much because whistling lowers the tone of the place but because it almost certainly signifies that thieves are exchanging messages: this or that shop is ripe for the plucking, is momentarily unattended, has a dozy or unwary assistant in charge. A similar plaque can be found at the rear of the Savoy Hotel in the Strand.

Admittedly, Johnson couldn't have known about the dangers of theft faced by the shopkeepers of Burlington Arcade, given that it was erected in 1819, which was getting on for forty years after his death; but as a glance at his poem, "London", confirms, he certainly knew about street gangs and the ways of city thieves, and he would therefore surely have known something of the use to which they put their ability to whistle. Whistling summoned them to action and it acted as a warning. Whistling had performed like services in earlier times, and it would do the same later. The writer Derrick Buttress remembers how as a boy on Nottingham's Broxtowe Estate in the 1930s he was called to take part in play or fighting by whistled signals that floated over house-tops sometimes from a distance of several streets. And as we shall see, the whistling shepherds of Aas, a village at the foot of the Pyrenees, put their expertise to good use during the Nazi Occupation of France.

II

Whistling as a call to arms or as the signal for dirty work afoot is a subject to be taken up later in this book. For the moment we need to return to the matter of the mechanics of whistling. How is it actually done? How *do* people learn to whistle, to be so articulate in making either by their own means or those of mechanical aids an enormously wide variety of sounds — from the shrill piping of a tiny bird to the deep sound of a steam whistle, from sweet melody to the blast of the Acme Thunderer, as a referee's whistle used to be called?

To start with unaided, purely human whistling. This isn't achieved merely by contracting the lips and blowing through them, that's for sure. The tongue is all-important. Its function seems in some senses analogous to how the reed operates in wind instruments, its vibrations helping to shape volume and pitch. Place the tip just behind the front teeth, raise and lower, push, withdraw, and by such means you create notation, make trills, warbles, pure notes. But lips and lungs are also involved in creating pitch and, more obviously, volume and sustainability of notes. Those who can whistle on an indrawn breath are able to achieve continuous whistling similar to the circular breathing that permitted such jazz musicians as Tommy Dorsey, Earl Bostick and Roland Kirk to blow without cease. Duke Ellington's baritone saxophonist, Harry Carney, was also a circular breather. At one New Year's gig, he ended his feature number, "Sophisticated Lady," by holding onto the last note for so long that the drummer eventually leant over to him. "I'm off now," he said. "See you same time next year." John Coltrane was yet another adept. Hence, his almost overwhelming fluency. "Man, I never know when to stop blowing," he once said within Miles Davis's hearing. "Try taking the horn out of your mouth," Miles suggested. Some whistlers seem to go on as long.

Although whistling, unlike playing the saxophone, may seem instinctive, it is nothing of the sort. Most people manage to whistle, a bit, but for anyone to become an accomplished whistler requires much practice. Of course, it doesn't seem like that. There are, it is true, some adjudicated whistling competitions, but for the most part whistlers — that is, the general public — are indifferent to or, more often, ignorant of them. To be a good whistler you don't need to sign up for a course on whistling — though in 20's California there was an Academy of Whistling and others may have existed — and there are no examination grades to bother about. You can practice any time, any place. It is free. Learning how to whistle is exciting as well as being an intensely pleasurable way of expressing yourself. But precisely because anyone can learn to whistle such music making is likely to be dismissed by class snobs and defenders of aesthetic "purity" as somehow not skilled. It isn't after all exclusive, it isn't sophisticated, it's "common," it isn't articulate. It's the sign of a vacant mind. Believe it if you will.

At the very least what whistling demonstrates is that most people have music in their souls. Through whistling you make music. Sweet music, too. As Orsino says to the disguised Viola in *Twelfth Night*, "thy small pipe/Is as the maiden's organ, shrill and sound." He means that her voice is a kind of musical instrument, pure, unbroken. She doesn't need to pipe a tune to be tuneful. No wonder the Japanese refer to anyone whistling as playing "the mouth flute." People will make music out of anything: oil drums, cigar boxes cut partially open with wires strung across to make a sound box, jugs over the lip of which you blow in order to make a deep note like a tuba, empty beer cans banged together, saws whose undulant blades make for a whiney, almost eldritch near-melody .... But nothing approaches whistling for accessibility, ease of articulation, and, above all, the sheer delight in making melody. It is the ultimate do-it-yourself music.

Which returns us once more to the question of how it's done. The entry on "Whistle" in the great 1911 edition of the *Encyclopaedia Britannica* is a considerable help. It defines the aural effect of whistling as "The shrill warbling sound made by forcing the breath through the lips, contracted to form a small orifice, or produced by any instrument of the whistle type; also, generically, any similar shrill, hissing or warbling sound, as of a bird's note, of wind through trees, ropes, &c." A brief etymological account of the word follows: "The O.Eng *hwistlian*, to whistle, and *hwistlere*, whistler, piper, are closely allied to *hwsiprian* or *hwaestrain*, to whisper, to speak softly under one's breath." Viola's small pipe is scarcely more than a whisper. And in the middle of the storm at the beginning of *Pericles*, the "the seaman's whistle is a whisper." (Act 1 scene iii).

The game of Chinese whispers is about inarticulacy, or anyway the risk of misunderstanding. But the mechanical whistle is made to

Photo by Leo Reynolds/The Januarist

articulate sounds. And, as the *Encyclopaedia* notes, it can take many forms: "from the straight flute and flageolet type made of wood or metal and pierced with holes, to the metal signalling pipe used for signalling on board or by policemen." Playing on the pipe or whistle requires finger-stopping and/or uncovering of the holes. This seems purely banausic, but watch any skilled piper and you will see with what dexterity their fingers hover, flitter across and over the holes so as to create trills, quavers of sounds, that are a distinctive feature of human whistling and produced by a combination of the tongue vibrating behind the front teeth and, sometimes, rapid, if slight, tightening and relaxation of the lips. Those ancestors of ours who made the first pipes were obviously trying to reproduce human whistling by mechanical means. *Ceci, c'est une pipe.*

Even to say this is to imply that playing on a pipe, learning to whistle articulately, is very different from merely putting your lips together in order to blow. "To blow the whistle" is to raise the alarm. As a mechanical action it is easily done. (As a moral one it is far more difficult. Whistle blowers frequently find themselves ostracised or worse.) When policemen were first sent out onto

England's streets in the 1830s they were issued with wooden rattles with which to signal their presence. But rattles are cumbersome. Besides, you don't really want to be chasing a criminal while whirring an instrument that sounds like a cicada with laryngitis. Soon enough, the rattles were got rid of and a policeman's lot made happier by the introduction of the whistle, which came about in the 1860s when Joseph Hudson invented and patented a whistle with an immediately recognisable, discordant note.

A manufactured whistle has a penetrative sound. The one Hudson came up with could be heard over a mile away. (Though, as we shall see, this is as nothing compared to the distances some trained whistlers can project their mouth whistling.) Still, to be able to send whistled sound an extended distance explains why mechanical whistles were adopted by railway guards, sports referees, and, during the second world war, ARP wardens, though wardens were issued with longer whistles whose distinctive sound had about it something of a treble organ note. No skill was or is required to blow any of these whistles. You simply put one to your lips and blow. A good thing, too. If you're intent on nabbing a burglar, or alerting train travellers as well as the driver to the fact that the train waiting at Platform Five is about to depart, or needing to warn people that uncurtained, lit windows can be direction-finders for enemy bombers, you certainly don't want to be bothered about where exactly to place your fingers or whether your embouchure is all it might be.

But pipers, whether at the gates of dawn or drawing to a close the midnight masquerade, have to be skilled performers. To call something a tin whistle or a penny flute may make it seem scarcely worthwhile, but to play one well requires not merely nimble fingers and a good pair of lungs. You also need a fine sense of rhythm and a good ear. These attributes are by no means as rare as some suppose. Many, perhaps most, people possess them. But learning how to put them to the best use takes time, practice, dedication. To repeat, anyone wanting to whistle well will spend countless hours learning

29

how to do it, and if this isn't recognised as assiduous practice it's only because there's no requirement to pay for tuition, nor to set aside an hour a day for such practice. Anyone can do it, any time, anywhere. Acquiring expertise as a whistler is open to all. You don't need a silver spoon in your mouth in order to learn how to whistle. In fact, before you can hope to whistle you have to get rid of the spoon. Only then can you make use of the motor and mental skills that whistling calls on, and this, whether using finger whistling, often in fact, three fingers thrust into the mouth, though only two are used for wolf whistling; or whistling with rounded, pursed lips, which is known to the cognoscenti as "sporgendo", a term we take from J.M. Schlitz, who wrote at some length about whistling as an art form.

To repeat, whistling is, with singing, the most democratic and universal of all forms of music making. According to Cloudesley Seddon, who began to write an account of whistling in the 1970s but who sadly died before he had got very far, "it is an intriguing fact that one can 'whistle for the moon' anywhere on earth but not on the moon. The first man to walk on the moon tried but failed!" Seddon knew this to be so, because he had contacted NASA to ask whether the astronauts who landed on the moon's surface tried to whistle while there. You can't fault him for lack of dedication to the cause. But the answer was disappointing. The atmospheric conditions of the moon, so Houston gravely informed him, made whistling impossible.

So, no whistling on the moon. But on earth it can and does happen just about anywhere, as does singing. Singing, though, can be made an exclusive art form. There are conservatoires for those wishing to be professional singers. Moreover, singing is gendered. Soprano voices are very different from those of basses. And singers are perforce required to sing the words of different languages. With the exception of the school in California referred to above — and that didn't last for long — none of this applies to whistling. You don't have an "educated" whistle, you don't possess a natural contralto whistle, and you don't whistle in German or Serbo-Croat, say. (Although, as a later chapter reveals, those who "speech whistle" do so in their respective languages.) You can, it is true, try to improve your whistling. Seddon recommends some exercises for those who wish to become proficient whistlers. Making a habit of deep breathing "morning and night" is one. Another is to practise to "keep the puckered lips taut and allow the tongue maximum flexibility for note production. The tongue is in a drawn-back position for low notes; tongue against bottom of lower teeth for middle scale, and close to upper edge of lower teeth for high notes." There are also exercises for what Seddon calls "waving, vibrato, trilling and yodelling effects," all of which are greatly helped if you "practice in front of a mirror." The mirror is especially useful for waving, which "demands a firm lower lip and jaw while the breath is emitted smoothly over an up-down-up-down movement of the tongue to produce closely connected notes alternately." But never mind if you lack the time, the jaw, and the mirror for all this. You're still free to whistle.

Beware, though, those who might mistake you for a madman or woman. In 1997 two whistlers returning on a cross-channel ferry to England from the continent discussed the possibility of setting up an English version of the German event, *Pfeifen im Walde,* which they had attended. The programme they discussed was nothing if not ambitious, and one of them, writing some time later from Switzerland to his English friend, made a suggestion as to how it

Alles pfeift und alle pfeifen, und fast niemand denkt darüber nach!
Das Festival Pfeifen im Walde stellt das Phänomen des Pfeifens in der Fülle seiner Facetten in den Mittelpunkt: als akustische und symbolische Äusserung bei Menschen und Tieren, in der Natur, in der Technik, als Teil der Alltagskultur, als Element der Musik. Das Pfeifen der Murmeltiere, Wale und Vögel, das Pfeifen des Weltalls, der Eisenbahn und Schiffahrt ist ebenso Gegenstand des Festivals wie populäre Pfeifmelodien und selten gehörte Volksmusik. Musik aus Zentralafrika und Amazonien, aus Sibirien, Japan, Laos und Albanien, aus dem Alpenraum und den Pyrenäen wird unter dem gemeinsamen Thema des Pfeifens mit klassischer europäischer Musik, neuer experimenteller Musik, pfeifender Kunst, Pfeifsprachen-Demonstrationen und Vogelstimmen-Imitationen zusammengeführt. Ein Filmprogramm, Workshops, ein internationales Symposium und der Grosse Wettbewerb der Amateurpfeifer, offen für die Luzernerinnen und Luzerner sowie die Gäste aus aller Welt, runden das Programm ab.

could be made more ambitious still. "*Eccentrics.* Don't take this wrong, but the British Isles have the highest percentage of eccentrics in the world. We should make a thorough search for whistling-related oddities in the dense underbrush of the lunatic fringe." And when found make a note of, as Captain Cuttle would say.

Whistle While
You Work

I

In his delightful, warmly appreciative biography of Edward Lear, written in the late 1930s, Angus Davidson quotes a letter Lear wrote about a chance encounter with some peasants while he was sketching in Albania. He thought he was doing no harm. They, on the contrary, thought he was about the Devil's work. "When I had sketched such of the principal buildings [of Elbassan] as they could recognise, a universal shout of 'Shaitan!' burst from the crowd; and strange to relate, the greater part of the mob put their fingers in their mouths and whistled furiously, after the manner of butcher-boys in England." (Penguin edn., 1950, p. 61.)

Davidson doesn't feel the need to explain that in more primitive communities — then, as still now — image-making was often regarded as a dangerous form of magic. (To take a photograph of someone is to steal that person's soul.) And Islamic countries have often taken a dim view of graven images, claiming it is against the Prophet's word. This disregards the great Islamic tradition of the visual arts, including 17th glassware with its exquisite decorative motifs of birds, animals, and flowers. But then all religions have, at different times and places, proscribed art.

Davidson sees no need to account for the Albanians' hostility to Lear's drawing. Nor does he feel any need to explain about butcher-boys. He assumes his readers will understand Lear's reference to the ferocity of their whistling. But it's a reasonable guess that few under the age of fifty will have heard the volume and pitch of whistling of which they, in common with other errand boys, were capable as they propelled their laden, heavy-duty bikes about town and village streets.

Whistling and work went together long before the streets were thronged with whistlers. Nor do whistling shepherds, whistling ploughmen, and other agricultural workers have to wait for John Clare to report their musical skills, though there's not much doubt that his accounts are the most frequent and perhaps evocative we have. For example, in "Rural Morning," Clare describes "Hodge"

> Prepared for Dobbin whom he means to ride
> The only tune he knows still whistling o'er
> And humming scraps his father sung before
> As 'wantley dragon' and the 'magic rose'
> The whole of music which his village knows
> That wild remembrance in each little town
> From mouth to mouth thro' ages handles down
> Onward he jolts nor can the minstrel throngs
> Entice him once to listen to their songs

The minstrel throngs are presumably birds at their own music. In sharp contrast to Clare himself, Hodge is indifferent to this bird song because he is intent on whistling and humming "the whole of music which his village knows." The songs which make this music, a kind of memory-stored library, are the "wild remembrance in each little town," where "wild" plays with "uncouth" in order to yield the richer meaning of untamed. In Letter V of *Fors Clavigera*, John Ruskin talks of witnessing a procession of agricultural workers as they follow a whistling steam engine — perhaps a threshing machine — whose attempt at an harmonious sound is a grotesquely comic version of the ploughmens' "thoughtless" whistling of earlier years, though the men themselves are so tired that they lack the energy to whistle. Ruskin doesn't suggest such whistling would

34

have been especially musical, let alone that it provided the melody of folk songs. But this is probably because he was unaware of the rich, stored tradition from which the songs came.

The songs the rural workers whistled are not the songs of polite tradition. They aren't the songs thought appropriate or anyway likely to be reproduced in the drawing-room, the kind that Jane Austen's heroines would have sung. These were almost entirely drawn from settings of Matthew Prior's verses plus 18th century sentimental songs and ballads, and were for the most part accompanied on the piano, often by the singer herself. They were evidence of leisure, of afternoon or evening entertainment for the gentry. They have nothing to do with a world of work. They were also ways of promoting marriageability. A sweet voice, an attractive profile, and — important, this — a white, curved but not muscular arm, were important desiderata in a potential wife.

The songs Clare mentions belong to a very different tradition, one handed down from generation to generation in a particular place and, no doubt, associated with the work done there. Everybody in that place could be expected to whistle the same tunes. They could whistle them when they were on their own. They could also whistle them in the certain knowledge that others hearing the melody would want to join in.

Not that communal whistling is confined to rural circumstance. Derrick Buttress remembers how Nottingham miners going on night shift would crowd onto the upstairs of buses and, through the beer and cigarette fug, wait for someone to begin whistling a tune that the others would then take up. "It could be deafening," Derrick says, "but it could also involve some miners whistling intricate harmonies on the main theme. It was sometimes great music that they made." And there's a scene in the 1942 film *Listen to Britain*, made by the Crown Film Unit to which more detailed reference will be made in the chapter on "Whistling as Entertainment," but which can be mentioned here because it features the music-hall singer-comedians Flanagan and Allen performing on the makeshift stage of a crowded works canteen. The two men sing "Sunnyside Lane," a variation of their great hit, "Underneath the Arches," then, having "stated the theme," as music books say, they fall silent while the entire audience begins to whistle the sweetly sentimental tune, one redolent of war-time nostalgia mingled with hope for not merely peace but that better future yearningly endorsed in Vera Lynn's "We'll Meet Again" and "There'll Be Bluebirds over the White Cliffs of Dover," tunes that must have been whistled by literally millions of Britons during the war years.

Communal whistling could also be a means of subverting or at least cocking a snook at authority. The poet Maurice Rutherford recalls how, as a young factory lad in the 1930s, he joined others in whistling a tune whenever a particularly unpopular foreman was on his rounds. "A Tisket, A Tasket" was a number popular at the time (Ella Fitzgerald's version made her instantly famous), but the reason the men at the factory whistled it was because the lyrics, slightly modified, ran "A tisket, a tasket/A little yellow BASKET." The workers put an especially emphasis on the two notes that signified "basket" (bastard), but, to adapt a famous army saying, no words, no pack-drill.

By the same token, women factory workers often flouted social stereo-typing, especially in war time. Dressed like men in overalls, they took on a jaunty independence or at least bolshie refusal to kow-tow unthinkingly to authority, and by derisive, mocking whistling frequently made clear their contempt for those who gave them their orders, especially men, the "Fancy Dans" with their clipboards and/or look of officialdom. Lawrence mocks this peacockery in *Sons and Lovers*, when he has Paul Morel strut around whistling as he tries to recover the jauntiness which has been badly wounded by Clara Dawes taking him down a peg or two.

Not that Clara herself whistles, but in later, wartime America, a woman factory worker, Dorothy Edwards by name, became a national emblem, when her whistling was regularly featured on radio programmes. She was apparently "discovered" while whistling as she laboured in the Lockheed Munitions Factory, and the sounds she made were thought to be a good cheer-up for a nation at war, though her radio work didn't spare her from the day job. She had to be rushed from factory to studio each time the programme was due to be aired.

II

There will be more to say about the whistling of industrial workers, but first, back to agriculture. As we noted earlier, workers in factories typically whistle *while* they work. Whistling, when it can be done, and isn't against the rules, helps the work go down, gives zest to mundane jobs, redeems routine and, especially where there are mixed workforces, can be a way of attracting attention, of flirting. More often, though, whistling is unselfconscious, at least to the extent that, as someone has observed, whistling and work go together as naturally as drawing breath. In his autobiography, published in 1852, Alexander Somerville, who identifies himself as "One Who Has Whistled at the Plough," records that "soon after six o'clock in the evening the ploughboys from the farm fields passed up this road with their horses on their way home from Branxton stables. One would sing; another would whistle." And for Robert Burns, whistling while he ploughed was a way of recalling and fixing in his memory melodies he needed for songs which he was composing. According to his early biographer, Lockhart, Burns would make himself "familiar with the traditional melody ... catch a suggestion from some fragment of old song ... fix upon an idea or situation for the new poem; then, humming or whistling the tune as he went about his work, he wrought out the new verses, going into the house to write them down."

But the whistling of those engaged in such work is also functional. They whistle *because* they work. Their whistling is intrinsic to their day-to-day lives. Shepherds whistle to their dogs when they need to give them instructions as to whether they should guard or lead the sheep to pasture, to pen, to protect them against coming storm. An outsider watching how a dog responds to the different whistled messages is likely to regard the understanding between man and animal as almost magical, but to the shepherds themselves it was and still is workaday routine. So, no doubt, are the whistles of the cowherd and all those who look after farmyard animals, including geese. So it must always have been. John Milton does not report the imparadised Adam as whistling, but it isn't difficult to imagine that he would have done so. He would have whistled for the joy of it.

Whistling can be the expression of contented absorption in work. The artist Eric Ravilious was an inveterate whistler and whenever a piece of work was going well his whistling, always sweetly ebullient, became, so those around him noticed, a series of ecstatic trills. Yet whistling can also be full of care, of concern. In the "Winter" section of *The Farmer's Boy,* the long poem which, when it was published in 1800, made its author, Robert Bloomfield, immediately famous, there is a reference to the swain who "whistles to his sheep," but although this form of communication belongs within the rural tradition, for the most part such whistling was directed at the shepherd's dog, reasonably enough. Dogs are more nimble than their masters, can race up a hill and down a valley, and, given their bark and bite, are more fearsome than a human. In his *Shepherd's Calendar,* Clare has some lines in the section on June where he remarks on the "shrill whistles" by which the shepherd guides his "barking dogs" to "Drive bleating sheep each morn from fallow fold."

Still, it is Bloomfield who writes intriguingly of how the farmer's boy, Giles by name, "join'd the various notes/Of nature's music from a thousand throats."

The Blackbird strove with emulation sweet
And echo answer'd from her close retreat

38

The sporting Whitethroat on some twig-end borne
Pourd hymns to freedom and the rising morn
Stopt in her turn perhaps the starting Thrush
Shook a bright shower from her Blackthorn-bush
Where dewdrops thick as early blossom hung
And trembld as the Minstrel sweetly sung.
(*The Farmer's Boy*, "Spring", lls 137-146)

This closely anticipates some lines in "Home Thoughts from Abroad", so much so that it's impossible not to think that Bloomfield's poem must have been lodged somewhere in Robert Browning's mind when he wrote of how the "blossomed pear-tree in the hedge/Leans to the field and scatters on the clover/Blossoms and dewdrops — at the bent sprays' edge —/That's the wise thrush".

But still more remarkable is Bloomfield's suggestion that the blackbird may "emulate" Giles's whistling. It has long been suggested that human whistling owes much to birdsong. Bloomfield, however, is saying that birdsong may be affected by human whistling, may copy it. Well, why not? The starling in particular is a famously good mimic of other bird song as well as of the human voice, and the same holds true for the jackdaw. As for blackbirds:

Do you know, Ian, I'm sometimes working in my back yard and I can hear my dad whistling. He's been dead for more than twenty years. When I look I see a blackbird. That bird's ancestors must have heard my dad's whistling and mimicked him. My dad's whistling has passed through a lot of eggs to get to that bird I hear now.

So, in *Bringing It All Back Home*, a memoir of working-class life in post-war Yorkshire, Ian Clayton reports a friend telling him. (Route Publishing, p. 320). The back yard was commonly a place for work:

for hammering segs into boots and shoes, for carpet beating, repairing items of furniture, for carpentry, for planting and tending flowers and veg. in tubs. Whistle while you work and teach the birds to whistle as you do.

This opens up territory that will be more fully explored in the chapter on Whistling as Communication. But it is relevant here to remark that rural occupation is for the most part solitary. Though agricultural workers come together at set times of the year — notably harvest — they are, and certainly were, more usually working alone. Whistling at your work creates a kind of symbiosis between man and bird. In the song "The Lark in the Morning" the lark is even regarded as a co-worker, for "like the pretty ploughboy she whistles and she sings/And goes home in the evening with the dew all on her wings."

That may be fanciful, but in *Men of the Tideway*, Dick Fagin's account of the Thames Lightermen (1966), the author tells us that he was required to learn what he believed to be the men's unique whistling signal, used when lightermen on the river needed to contact others. "I ought to explain," he says, "that every lighterage firm had its own kind of whistle — the sound, I mean, because all the whistling was done with the mouth and not with any instrument. Whistling was a way of identifying yourself across distances, especially at night, with other men working for the same company. Very useful. Getting it right was a work of art, though." Sometime later, when Fagin had got it right, and was strolling along the river bank with a girl friend, he was amazed to hear exactly the same whistling made by a blackbird. But which whistle had come first? Who had learnt from whom? Who is attracting whose attention?

A tinker striding across country most certainly wants to attract attention by his whistling. It's the sure way to alert housewives to his approach. "As merry as a tinker." It was the whistling that made him merry. Tinkers had a reputation for being ladies' men. Their whistling brought women to their doors and, maybe, an invitation to enter. (The bawdy meaning of whistle, the phallus, seems to be part

Brown and silver: Old Battersea Bridge,
Thames lightermen painting by James Abbott Whistler

of their merriness.) But whatever licence the whistling might imply,
it was nevertheless as functional as that of two-tone ice-cream van.

Of course, tinkers weren't confined to rural England. They also
plied their trade in towns. When, as a young boy I (JL) lived in the
Leicestershire village of Burbage, we were all familiar with a local
character, "Whistling Billy," who in dry weather slept in an old
bath under a spinney hedge, and in times of wet and cold made his
bed in Farmer Record's barn. Billy was sometimes called a tramp
but he was by trade a tinker who could be found walking the streets
of nearby towns, Hinckley and Sapcote. And there was a rumour
that he occasionally journeyed as far as Leicester, where he could
be spotted whistling up business.

Tinkers were essentially roamers, like other itinerant workers
and Gypsies. All were whistlers and their whistling is inevitably
connected to and even expressive of work in pre-industrial

41

England. "The Carman's Whistle" is an old ballad which celebrates the attentive ways of carters whose care for their horses was such that, as one commentator noted, "if the carman's horse be melancholy or dull with heavy and hard labour, then will he like a kind piper, whistle him a fit of mirth to any tune; of which generosity and courtesy your coachman is altogether ignorant, for he never whistles, but all his music is to rap out an oath." (John Taylor, "The Water Poet"). This observation is corroborated by the Elizabethan writer and dramatist, Henry Chettle, who reported that the carman was "was wont to whistle to his beasts a comfortable note."[1]

Carmen or carters, like brewers' draymen with their barrels of ale, were for many centuries a common sight in the streets of England, their wagons shifting heavy loads, household goods, pieces of machinery, building materials. They were also known for their abilities as whistlers. Ploughmen similarly whistled to their teams, instructing them to make a turn at the end of the field, urging them to keep straight along the furrow, but also whistling to give them pleasure. The measure of regard between farmer-worker and his horse explains the desolation so many men felt when, during the Great War, millions of horses — as many as 9,000,000 according to one estimate — whom the men regarded as their work companions were sent to the Western Front, from where they never returned. France became their graveyard. They were blown to pieces, injured beyond recovery, starved, drowned in mud, broken by the effort to haul monstrously heavy gun carriages across cratered fields. During the 1930s a retired ploughman in the Vale of Belvoir was sometimes invited into junior schools in the area to talk of the changing nature of rural occupation. A woman from the Vale remembered all her life the tears in the old man's eyes as he told the children about the horses, many of whose names he could recite, who were taken from their farm work at Bottesford to what became the killing fields of Western Europe. After the war, he told the children, he never again felt like whistling.

III

When we turn to work in industrial times, we find that, as mentioned in the Introduction, whistling may be understandably prohibited (in the mines, backstage at the theatre) and less excusably frowned on. ("Don't whistle your work away.") True, the heavy clatter of factory machines may make whistling impossible because inaudible, but whistling was anyway disliked by factory overseers who, as Dickens said, seemed to be hired "to depress the spirits of the people." And these people were for the most part ones who still retained links with the rural tradition where whistling was an intrinsic part of work and social life. Many industrial workers in the early to mid-nineteenth century were first generation town and city workers. For one reason or another — enclosure, low wages, agricultural depression — they left the land for industrial labour. Others were the children of former agricultural workers. Whistling was common to them. But though they could and did whistle about the streets, they were far less likely to whistle at work. Conditions discouraged whistling. So did factory rules.

The psychological and emotional damage the loss of music entailed for such workers plainly can't be quantified. But social historians such as G.E. Mingay who have used this in order to dismiss the claim of this damage or have argued that it was compensated for by regular work and steady wages are, quite simply, contemptible. For all the criticisms levelled against those great pioneers of Labour History, the Hammonds, they are much closer to a true understanding of the human cost involved in industrialisation than are any of their opponents. As they say, anyone wanting to reach a proper assessment of this cost must "remember that the population that was flung into the brutal rhythm of the factory had earned its living in relative freedom ... and that the early factory was particularly savage. No economist of the day, in estimating the gains and losses of factory employment, ever allowed for the strain that a man suffered in his feelings as he passed from a life where he could eat, or dig or sleep as he pleased, to one in which somebody turned the key on him and for fourteen hours a day he had not even the right to whistle."

Say if you will that the Hammonds sentimentalise the working man's right to dig or sleep as he pleased — oh, no he couldn't, not if the farmer wanted him out of his tied cottage. The fact remains that the new conditions at the very least curtailed a sense of freedom. At worst, they made miserable many working lives. Nor were the Hammonds being fanciful in mentioning that factory "hands" were forbidden to whistle. (And how that word "hands" tells of the way in which, as Ruskin remarked, workers were thought of as reducible to their functional parts.) In his *Condition of the Working Class in England in 1844* Engels, who is scaldingly ironic about operatives having "a mission to be bored every day" from their eighth year, quotes the various factory rules laid down for weavers, including the one that "Every operative detected speaking to another, singing or whistling, will be fined 6d." No argument was to be tolerated as to whether the whistling had been truly "detected." Engels reports that one newly appointed supervisor was "dismissed for fining too little; and so bringing in five pounds too little weekly." Not good enough a snooper, too decent a human being, perhaps.

There's a sadistic cruelty in denying workers the right to sing and whistle. Besides, you wouldn't bother to forbid this urge to make melody if only a few were inclined to it. One or two whistling and singing hardly matters. We can be reasonably sure that most if not all the operatives wanted to find ease from their mind-numbing, physically arduous work in making music. And for this they were to be fined by the joyless, punitive, pettifogging Bounderbys of the cotton-mill industry, though in fact the ban on whistling begins with Josiah Wedgwood in the 1780s and runs through to Henry Ford's assembly lines. Ford instructed all department heads to ban any whistling or talking. Such signs of human expressiveness weren't conducive to efficient work. Ironic to think that thousands of Ford's workers must have seen the Disney film, *Snow White and*

44

the *Seven Dwarfs*, which was released in 1937, extolling the pleasures of whistling while you worked. It's when you consider the implications of the ban on whistling at the workplace that you begin to take the measure of Dickens's deep loathing of all that he had in his sights when he sat down to write *Hard Times*. A society from which all pleasure, all individuality, were to be erased. "Every operative detected speaking to another, singing or whistling, will be fined 6d." Ironic also that in the Depression years advertisers in the USA were quick to seize on whistling as a token of the freedoms enjoyed in a capitalist society.

IV

Nor was a ban on whistling confined to factory workers.

> And there you'll see the gardeners, the men and 'prentice boys
> Told off to do as they are bid and do it without noise;
> For, except when seeds are planted and we shout to scare the birds,
> The Glory of the Garden it abideth not in words.
> ("The Glory of the Garden.")

True, Rudyard Kipling is writing metaphorically. Englishmen don't go around making a fuss about what they have accomplished. But the metaphor would make no sense if it didn't take for granted that labourers in the garden that is England shouldn't whistle their work away. And although in "The Song of the Banjo," Kipling has his musician declare that he can "rip your heartstrings out" with "The tunes that mean so much to you alone —/Common tunes that make you choke and blow your nose —/Vulgar tunes that bring the laugh that brings the groan" (ah, the potency of cheap music), these tunes have no right to be heard in the workplace, wherever that may be, in country or town.

Just so, the sign at the back of the Savoy in the Strand, forbidding whistling, while in part intended to alert would-be thieves to the management's presence, also served to warning employees against making unseemly sounds. House-servants, in particular, were forbidden to whistle, however large or small the house they served in. Virginia Woolf's Mrs Dalloway is exceptional in feeling only pleasure in her house's "familiar veils and the response to old devotions. The cook whistled in the kitchen. She heard the click of the typewriter. It was her life, and bending her head over the hall table, she bowed beneath the influence, felt blessed and purified." Perhaps the fact that Mrs Walker "was Irish and whistled all day long," made her incorrigible.

But for the most part, cooks wouldn't have dared to whistle. Nor would shop assistants. The maternal grandmother of one of the present authors started life as a counter-assistant in a milliners' shop in Kenilworth, his paternal grandmother was an "under-maid" at a big house in Torquay, and neither could reconcile themselves to the sound of whistling about the house. Whistling was vulgar, the former

under-maid said, in the words of the other it was "not at all nice." And no doubt their censure was shared by the employers of those who worked in the service industries.

Whistling and work could of course go together in less regimented occupations, ones where you weren't subject to scrutiny, or were in the fortunate position of being self-employed. Blacksmiths were famous whistlers. Postmen, milkmen, bakers on their rounds, all whistled, in Britain at all events, though the "American Messenger Service," before it became the United Parcel Service, issued instructions that all postmen and post boys had to wear uniforms and agree "to abide by a strict code of behaviour, including courtesy to customers and no whistling." But out of sight, out of hearing.

On the other hand, Toodle, the cheerful fireman-stoker of whom Dickens makes a good deal in *Dombey and Son,* actually wants his whistle to be heard. So he should, of course. For a whole variety of reasons, people need to know that a train is approaching. But

Toodle means more than that. At one point he advises his children on how they can best live. They "can't be better than to be open," he says. "If you find yourselves in cuttings or in tunnels, don't you play no secret games. Keep your whistles going, and let's be hearing from you." Admittedly, Toodle has a steam whistle in mind, but his funny, lovely metaphor confirms that the whistler, confident of being heard, has nothing to hide. Being of good cheer is being beyond any possible recrimination, is being clean as a whistle.

A tunnel provides excellent acoustics for a whistle. So does an empty room. The painters and decorators in Robert Tressell's *Ragged-Trousered Philanthropists* aren't allowed to whistle, though they inevitably make a good deal of noise. There is the "hammering and sawing, the ringing of trowels, the rattle of pails, the splashing of water brushes," but no whistling. Whistling does, though, feature, albeit briefly, in Arnold Bennett's *Anna of the Five Towns,* where the house being prepared for the newly-married Anna, having been stripped of its old furniture, is invaded by plasterer, painter and paper hanger, who "whistled and sang in it."

Toodle isn't described as doing his own whistling. The engine he stokes is, though, an extension of his energy, even his dauntless determination to live a good life. There is an extra meaning lurking in his words. Whistling in the dark is a way of keeping your courage up. Clare has several references to Helpstone villagers slipping past reputedly haunted places in their locality, whistling as they go. And the haunted Peter Grimes, in George Crabbe's great poem, has three places he fears to approach. "When he drew near them he would turn from each,/And loudly whistle till he passed the reach."

But Toodle's principal intention is to encourage his children to be as clean as a whistle. And behind that idiomatic phrase is another. The man or woman who is clean, whose work is beyond reproof, is "worth the whistle." No wonder Baden Powell insisted that "a good scout whistles and smiles all the time," though as

Maurice Rutherford has drily remarked, "I could do both, but never at the same time."

V

Men working on their own, the cottage frame-weavers, for example, sang at their tasks. They may even have smiled. They certainly whistled. It was common practice for cottagers to keep song birds in cages, which they hung in the parlour and, in summer, outside the cottage door. The majority of such birds were native — robins and, especially, linnets — but Henry Mayhew reports on the huge trade of birds brought in from Germany for this purpose. According to him, imported bullfinches "have been chiefly taught to sing by weavers whilst at work at their looms, which is said to account for the birds beginning to sing when the head of a person standing before [it] is moved backwards and forwards." By "sing" Mayhew obviously means here "whistle."

This extends a remark of Gilbert White's, that "It is pretty evident that the Germans, who bring vast numbers of [bullfinches] to London which they have taught to pipe, must have instructed them more by whistling to them, than by the organ." But then, as this form of work was supplanted by large mill-factories, the terrible clatter of machinery made whistling all but impossible — or anyway pointless. As a result whistling when away from work — coming and going — became a preoccupation. It must also, even if tacitly, have signified freedom. Consciousness, *pace* Engels, wasn't entirely defined on or by the factory floor.

As for those whose labour belonged to and with independent traders, freedom was even more relished. To the butcher-boys whose shrill, loud whistling was noted by Edward Lear, can be added all the others: bakers, grocers, and, later, the telegram boys who, during the Great War, were told not to whistle when cycling to the many thousands of households across the country where their visits were dreaded because the telegrams inevitably brought news of a son or husband killed in action.

But elsewhere, whistling was the norm. "When I worked on Hull's fish dock/market," Maurice Rutherford writes, "everybody whistled: the 'bobber' who unloaded the trawlers, barrowlads, filleters, rullymen, [drivers of horse-drawn drays which carried a load of 10-stone "kits" of fish from market to the salting farms] all whistled and, surely, under the conditions in which some of them worked, not because they were HAPPY."

VI

Which brings us back to the dark side of whistling. You might whistle while you worked, but whistling could also put you off work. Sometimes whistling acted as — could be interpreted as — an omen, a warning of coming disaster, though such whistling didn't usually proceed from the lips of the living. The only exception is of "whistling down the wind," which is when someone's reputation is slandered. You defame character by whistling for the wind to blow it away. It is, of course, the wind that does the work, and presumably it whistles derisively as it bears off the person's good name.[2]

Ominous whistling might come from birds. Hence, the Seven Whistlers. Seven is the number most frequently associated with magic events or phenomena. Seven lean years, seven hills of Rome, seven sleepers, seven wise men, seven liberal arts, seven wise virgins .... Nevertheless, there is a haunting power in the following story, reported in *The Leicester Chronicle* on 24th March, 1855.

> On Friday, the 16th inst. a collier ... was asked by a tradesman ... why he was not at his usual work. The reply ... was that none of the men had gone to work ... because they had heard the 'Seven Whistlers,' ... birds sent by Providence to warn them of an impending danger, and ... when they heard that signal not a man would go down the pit

The tradesman apparently suggested that this was mere superstition. Not so, the miner replied. The Seven Whistlers had previously been heard twice, the colliers who heard them had defied the warning they brought, went down the pit, "and two lives were lost on each occasion."

Were the whistlers birds? Not originally, it seems. According to a Leicestershire legend, "seven colliers got drunk on Sunday and towards nightfall decided to whistle as a wager to pay for more drink. They were instantly whisked up into the clouds by a whirlwind. Each night, as darkness falls, they 'fly from place to place, when fatal accidents are impending, to warn … their survivors to avoid their own terrific and never-dying destiny.'" This is a muddle, although sense can be made of it if we assume that some sort of freak accident happened to the seven drunken miners: a heavy wind blowing a tree or wall down on them, perhaps. Drinking, especially on a Sunday, could certainly be thought of as deserving God's displeasure. As for whistling for more drink: Brewer, as previously noted, offers as explanation of the phrase "to whistle for more": "In the old whistle-tankards, the whistle comes into play when the tankard is empty, to announce to the drawer that more liquor is wanted. Hence the expression, If a man wants liquor *he must whistle for it.*"

But the legend of the Seven Whistlers spread wider than the midlands or the work of miners. Men engaged in other dangerous callings also heard them. Frank Buckland, author of the classic work, *The Natural History of British Fishes* (1891), reports a story he heard from an old fisherman in Folkestone in the middle years of the 19th century, who feared the sound of overhead whistling on stormy nights. He attributed such whistling to birds of ill omen.

There's always an accident when they comes. I heard 'em once one dark night last winter. They come over our heads all of a sudden, singing 'ewe-ewe,' and the men on the boat

wanted to go back. It came on to rain and blow soon afterwards... and sure enough before morning, a boat was upset,
and seven poor fellows drowned.

The birds were identified as "long-billd curlews"; elsewhere the
Seven Whistlers are linked to different species of bird: swifts, teal,
widgeon, and golden plover. But as Jennifer Westwood and
Jacqueline Simpson, from whom all this information comes, rightly
remark, "knowing that birds made the noise is not the same thing as
ascribing their advent to natural causes." (*Country Lore and
Legends*, Penguin, 2005.)
    And finally in a section dealing with whistling and disaster we
should remember the whistling of the Death-in-Life Woman in
"The Rhyme of the Ancient Mariner," whose "lips are red", so
Coleridge tells us, whose "skin is white as leprosy," and who is "far
liker Death than he,/Her flesh makes the still air cold.." Most inter-
preters of the poem see her as an allegory of syphilis. She plays the
mariners at dice and — "The Game is done! I've won, I've
won!"/Quoth she, and whistled thrice." Her whistling presages the
mariners' deaths.

Four times fifty living men
  With never a sigh or groan,
With heavy thump, a lifeless lump
  They dropp'd down one by one.

VII

Leave ominous whistling aside. The urge to whistle, to make music,
seems to be a constant and to survive most work experiences. And
when permitted, it enhances them. Whistling is, or anyway was, infectious. Workers on building sites would take up the tune whistled by
one of them, "like a Mexican wave," one recalls. Miners who couldn't

51

whistle at the coal face made up for that by whistling virtually every-where else, not merely on the upstairs of buses. "You could whistle going down in the cage," an old miner told his niece, "you could whistle coming up, and while you were down you could whistle in order to guide the pit ponies to the shaft bottom", from where the coal they had hauled would be taken to the surface, "but that was it."

But even without whistling companions, men whistled while they worked, as though it was an essential part of the creativity they brought to whatever work they turned to. In *Sons and Lovers* Lawrence writes of how Walter Morel whistles while he works at home. His wife, Lawrence says, "lay listening to him tinkering away in the garden, his whistling ringing out as he sawed and hammered away. It always gave her a sense of warmth and peace to hear him thus as she lay in bed, the children not yet awake, in the bright, early morning, happy in his man's fashion." (Part 1, chapter 1.) Morel's happiness is mediated through his wife's consciousness, but this doesn't in any way diminish or belittle it. On the contrary, the "bright, early morning" evokes a sense of innocent delight before, for both man and woman, the troubles of the day come back.

On the way to or from the mines, in their pubs, and at home, in and out of doors, the miners, like other working men and women, whistled. Maurice Rutherford is no doubt right when he says that he can't imagine that all the men who whistled on Hull's dockside were especially happy. But whistling was the place they could go to in order to assert or find happiness, if, by that, we mean freedom from the workaday world by which otherwise they were bound.

This, though, abuts on whistling as self-expression and so belongs to the next chapter. But whistling as the sign of absorption in work — Morel's kind of whistling — is attendant on agricultural work quite as much as industrial labour. Yes, the whistling of agricultural workers often has a purpose. But not only that.

There was Huw Puw, too. What shall I say?
I have heard him whistling in the hedges

On and on, as though winter
Would never again leave those fields,
And all the trees were deformed. ("On the Farm.")

The Welsh farm labourer of R.S. Thomas's poem doesn't whistle in
joy, but the sounds signify a habit of work which, while certainly not
joyous, nevertheless testify to a stubborn persistence, an ability to
endure.

By way of closing this chapter, then, it seems appropriate to refer
to a story "Whistling Dick," by the American writer, O. Henry.
Henry writes that the tune his eponymous protagonist, a rail-riding
hobo, whistles, "followed an air, but it swam mistily into a swirling
current of improvisation. You could cull out the trill of mountain
brooks, the staccato of green rushes shivering in chilly lagoons, the
pipe of sleepy birds." This is not merely to evoke nature's music, it's
a particular kind of nature, one remote from the smoky, crowded
city. In particular, it's the opposite of anti-melodic, mechanical and
"appalling toots" of an "industrious tug."

But Whistling Dick runs up against Fritz, the policeman, a
known antagonist he's hoping to avoid but who is led to him
because Dick can't stop whistling. Most of us, at least those of a
certain age, are occasionally startled to find ourselves whistling. As
suggested earlier in this chapter, the music seems unselfconscious,
inadvertent, the whistling begun without us, so to speak. That's how
it is for Dick. Fortunately for him, Big Fritz takes a comparatively
charitable view of his quarry's behaviour, though he can't resist
pointing out that were it not for his leniency Dick could have ended
up "in a gage to wistle mit der chail birds," and having delivered
himself of this piece of grim humour, he feels himself entitled to
reprove the hobo when at one moment Dick is whistling a wrong
note, by which he means that he whistles a variation on the
"correct" tune.

Significantly, red-headed Dick is Irish, Fritz, as his name makes
evident, German, and the place they come together is New Orleans.

Rebelliousness and the law operate in an uneasy equipoise in the city of "Sporting House girls ... balconies and quadrilles/Everyone making love and going shares." Fritz, that stickler for correctness, is a man of the law, of uniform. Whistling Dick, on the other hand, is an escapee from time's burdens. Whistling for him is an expression of freedom. It signifies his independence of the cage of work, a rejection of daily obedience to laws he never made. And to say this leads us to the next chapter.

Notes

[1] Dinka tribesmen are, or anyway were, well-known for the way in which they whistled, sang, and spoke to their animals. It is likely that such behaviour is very widely spread.

[2] Older cinema goers will perhaps remember the film *Whistle Down the Wind*, released in 1961 and starring Alan Bates and Hayley Mills (the daughter of Mary Hayley Bell, on whose story the film was based.) The story is about three children who believe an escaped murderer they come upon and help to hide is in fact Jesus Christ, a belief they persuade their friends to share. The title is intriguingly ambiguous, and the film, for all the story's seeming improbability, is still well worth watching. An unmemorable musical version of *Whistle Down the Wind* was staged in 1996.

Whistling as Self-Expression

I

Whistling is a human activity. This may seem obvious to the point of triteness but it makes for a good joke. In the 1987 pilot episode of *Star Trek: The Next Generation,* which is called "Encounter at Farpoint," whistling is shown to be beyond the reach of androids. Commander Data tries to whistle "Pop Goes the Weasel," in order to show that he is capable of becoming a human, but he can't do it. Three years later, in the episode "Brothers," by which time he has learnt to pat his head and rub his stomach simultaneously, he is no further forward in acquiring skill as a whistler, and in the final episode, "Nemesis," produced in 2001, while he is now human in all others respects, whistling is still beyond him.

Tough on androids. Because, Norman Lewis's Yemenis apart, whistling seems intrinsic to human expression. Damn braces, bless relaxes. Whistling can be a way of asserting or pretending to relaxation. A routine of film or stage comic business involves a character under well-founded suspicion of having committed a minor misdemeanour gazing around or at his feet or up to the heavens while he whistles. Not me, squire. You're looking for the wrong man. I'm clean as a whistle. An odd phrase, that. Neither Brewer nor Partridge has it, and the disappointing *Oxford Book of Idioms,* while correctly explaining that "clean as a whistle" means "extremely clear" and "free of incriminating evidence," doesn't account for it. It may be an example of circular meaning. I whistle to show I'm innocent, have an untroubled conscience. How do you know I'm innocent? Because I whistle.

Whistling to demonstrate a clear conscience is the burden of Jiminy Cricket's song in Disney's *Pinocchio*. "Give a little whistle," he advises the puppet, when you're sure you know right from wrong, "and always let your conscience be your guide." Such saccharine morality is some distance from the innocent exuberance of "There chanced to pass a whistling boy/Whistling a tune in childish joy," and joy or exuberance are qualities the Romantic poets, from Blake to Clare, celebrate in many of their references to whistling.

Before we go further with this account of whistling as self-expression or self-communing or self-reflection — by all or any of which phrases we could have named the present chapter — we need, however, to repeat what was said in the Introduction, that traditionally whistling is a male activity. Only disreputable women whistled. It's at least possible that one reason for calling prostitutes "nightingales," a use which Partridge traces to no earlier than the mid-19th century, is that they came out in the evening and whistled up custom. In his *Dictionary of Phrase and Fable*, Brewer, having quoted the saying about a whistling woman and crowing hen being no good for god or men, explains that "A whistling maid means a witch, who whistles like the Lapland witches to call up the winds; they were supposed to be in league with the devil." (In some Asian cultures whistling inside the house by women is condemned because it is thought to summon spirits who may bring harm to the occupants.) Brewer adds that "The crowing of a hen was supposed to forbode death" — presumably because it was linked to Peter's betrayal of Christ, "Before the cock crows thrice."

Finally, Brewer remarks that the usual interpretation of the saying is that "masculine qualities in females are undesirable." Stradlater, the all-American he-man in J.D. Salinger's *The Catcher in the Rye*, and someone who is deeply in love with himself, has, so Holden Caulfield reports, "one of those very piercing whistles that was practically never in tune, and he always picked out some song that's hard to whistle even if you're a good whistler, like 'Song of India' or 'Slaughter on Tenth Avenue'. He could really mess a song up." Not that Stradlater would care. He especially enjoys whistling while he's shaving. He looks in the mirror and likes what he sees. His whistling is a form of bully-boy self-assertiveness. Here I am. Pretty good, hey? No woman should ever be like that. No woman should want to draw attention to herself. Modesty forbids.

This has relevance to another version of the rhyme: "Whistling women and outcast men/Will never come to any good end." Outcast men are likely to be vagabonds and tramps, whistlers all, and disreputable. Whistling women may be Gypsy women, themselves therefore vagabonds and tramps, outcasts from respectability. Steven Neeston, dog-trainer and former shepherd whose expertise will be referred to in a later chapter, remembers that in Co. Donegal where he grew up in the 50s, whistling in a girl was thought so reprehensible that one caught in the act was ordered to immediate Confession. "The Blessed Virgin will be hanging her head in shame," the girl at fault was told. This confirms a remark of Edna O'Brien's, that as a girl growing up in Catholic Ireland "you tried to whistle," but were stopped by religious convention.

But you didn't have to be a Catholic to feel as a woman the disapproval of society at your giving way to whistling. A telling chapter in *Tess of the D'Urbervilles* reveals Hardy's subtle understanding of how for a woman — especially a young woman — whistling as private delight can, if overheard by a man, become charged with unwanted significance. Tess is brought before her elder kinswoman Mrs d'Urberville, who asks her

"Can you whistle?"
"Whistle, ma'am?
"Yes, whistle tunes."

Tess could whistle, like most other country girls, though the accomplishment was one which she did not care to profess in company.

57

However, she blandly admitted that such was the fact.

"Then you will have to practise it every day. I had a lad who did it very well, but he has left. I want you to whistle to my bullfinches...."

So Tess, who hasn't for some time whistled, goes out into the garden and, thinking she is on her own, tries to re-learn, "wondering how she could have so grown out of the art which had come by nature."

But then she realises that she is being spied on by Mrs d'Urberville's son, Alec. He offers to teach her, tells her to try again.

Tess was quite serious, painfully serious by this time; and she tried —ultimately and unexpectedly emitting a real round sound. The momentary pleasure of success got the better of her; her eyes enlarged, and she involuntarily smiled in his face.

Entirely innocent though this is, she instinctively senses that Alec is bound to misread both whistling and her smile as carrying a sexual charge, so she stops.

She soon found that whistling to the bullfinches in Mrs d'Urberville's room was no such onerous business when she had regained the art, for she had caught from her musical mother numerous airs that suited those songsters admirably. A far more satisfactory time than when she practised in the garden was this whistling by the cages each morning. Unconstrained by the young man's presence she threw up her mouth, put her lips to the bars, and piped away in easeful grace to the attentive listeners.

Alec, however, isn't easily shaken off. One day, when Tess is whistling to the bullfinches, she has the impression "that the toes of a pair of boots were visible below the fringe of the curtain.

Thereupon her whistling became so disjointed that the listener, if such there were, must have discovered her suspicion of his presence." (Chapter 9.) "If such there were" — it seems an odd phrase, given that the sentence concludes by more or less acknowledging Alec's intrusive presence. But the point is that Tess's pleasure in whistling depends on privacy. Nor is it disapproval she most fears. The merest hint of a man's presence, especially a man whom she senses is sexually rapacious, is enough to destroy her pleasure in making music.

Hardy's delicate handling of Tess's delight in whistling and her keen sense that its being thought socially inappropriate is, in the true sense, unnatural — for she has come by her art "by nature" — tells much of conventional assumptions and prejudices, and in particular of how women's whistling was interpreted in the 19th century. (Prejudices and interpretations that lingered into the 20th century.) And it is therefore a nice irony that the men who whistle for pleasure in Dickens' novels are men of natural good feeling, womanly men, you might say, whereas manly women are opposed to whistling. In *Dombey and Son*, Mr Chick's almost compulsive whistling draws reproofs from his wife, that tight-laced woman who, as befits the sister of Dombey, is positively rigid with propriety, and who takes a dim view of her husband's tendency to put his hands in his pockets "and to whistle and hum tunes," although, "sensible of the indecorum of such sounds in a house of grief [this is after the first Mrs Dombey's death], he was at some pains to repress" the instinctive sounds that come from his lips. So that when he attempts to excuse his whistling as "mere habit", his wife retorts, "Nonsense! Habit! ... If you're a rational being don't make such ridiculous excuses. Habit! If I was to get a habit (as you call it) of walking on the ceiling, like the flies, I should hear enough of it, I dare say." (Chapter 2.)

Mr Chick's lamentable failure to achieve rationality is revealed in Phiz's illustration of "The Christening Party." This takes place on "an iron-grey autumnal day," and in the illustration the

The Christening Party

infant Paul Dombey is shown being complacently stared at by Dombey, who "represented in himself the wind, the shade, and the autumn of the christening." Meanwhile, Mr Chick, lips pursed, is either doing his damnedest not to whistle or has given way to the impulse. The text isn't specific, but Dickens does say that Mr Chick "really liked" Florence, Paul's unregarded sister, that he "showed that he liked her, and was about to show it in his own way now, when Paul cried, and his helpmate stopped him short." (Chapter 5.) Perhaps Mr Chick wanted to communicate fellow-feeling to another sufferer under Dombey's oppressive pride. But any reader is bound to consider that a burst of whistling, expressive of Mr Chick's innate kindliness, would also have enlivened this otherwise frozen occasion.

There is no way of knowing whether Disney intended Snow White's song "Whistle While You Work," to be an ersatz act of defiance against what was considered respectable for women. Her work is, after all, purely domestic. The dwarves go off to work down the diamond mine, taking the tools of their trade with them — shovel, pick, hammer, spade, lantern — and whistling as they go. Presumably, they have to stop whistling once they are down there. Snow White meanwhile gets on with domestic chores, and the tools of *her* trade are broom and duster. But less than a hundred years earlier it wasn't thought proper for women to whistle even in the comfort of their own homes. In Louisa May Alcott's *Little Women* (1868) Jo, the tomboy rebel, is accused by one of her sisters of using "slang words." Jo's response is to ape boyishness by putting her hands in her pockets and beginning to whistle.

"Don't Jo; it's so boyish."
"That's why I do it."
"I detest rude, unladylike girls."
"I hate affected, niminy-piminy chits."

This interchange, quoted in Julia Coleman's splendid *The Life of Slang* (OUP, 2012, p. 192) shows both the conventional mid-nineteenth century view that whistling is not for women and, at the same time, allows women readers to side with Jo's protest against niminy-piminy chits.

II

Still, men are or anyway were far more likely to be seen and heard as whistlers. The work they did while they whistled was carried out in public places: fields, streets, building plots. Whether they walked, rode — on horse-back, carts, bicycles — or stood at their labour, they were as audible as they were visible. And their whistling was an assertion of selfhood. There is a fine example of this in *King Lear*. Regan and her husband, the Duke of Cornwall, order Kent to be placed in the stocks. Gloucester offers to "entreat" for him, but Kent tells him not to bother. He is, he says, inured to hardship. "I have watch'd and travell'd hard;/Some time I shall sleep out, the rest I'll whistle." (Act 2, scene ii). "Watch'd" here means "gone without sleep." Kent has been travelling in order to watch over his master. Having been banished by Lear, he travels in disguise, presumably as some sort of mendicant, or, though the term wasn't then in existence, hedge-scholar. When, after Kent's return to England, Lear first encounters and fails to recognise his faithful follower and asks who and what he is, Kent replies that his profession is "to love him that is honest; to converse with him that is wise, and says little; to fear judgement; to fight when I cannot choose; and to eat no fish." (Act 1, scene iv). Judgement is here both earthly and heavenly. Kent presents himself as a travel-hardened commoner who may have to fight to save himself from harm, and who as a meat-eater is no milksop. (Though his abjuring of fish may also be intended to imply that he is a good Protestant.) And as someone used to keeping his own company he will whistle.

Shakespeare's Antony is also forced to keep his own company when, in Enobarbus's report, Cleopatra takes to the water in her royal barge. The entire city, we are told, "cast/Her people out upon her; and Antony,/Enthroned i' th' market-place, did sit alone,/Whistling to th' air; which but for vacancy,/Had gone to gaze on Cleopatra too,/And made a gap in nature." (Act 2, scene iii). The whistling is Shakespeare's own addition. His source,

Plutarch's *Lives of the Noble Greek and Romans*, "Englished" by Sir Thomas North, says only that "Antonius was left post alone in the market-place, in his imperial seat to give audience." Shakespeare's genius lies in that small, humanising touch of Antony's "Whistling to th' air." It tells of enforced loneliness, of Antony's having, for all his greatness as a Roman soldier and triple pillar of the world, to idle the time away until Cleopatra deigns to come to him. Of course, whistling in such circumstances is also a way of keeping up appearances, of feigning an insouciance we know Antony doesn't actually feel. He wants his Egyptian dish.

A rather similar form of whistling engages the attention of Dick Swiveller in Dickens's early masterpiece, *The Old Curiosity Shop*. Dick is a comic take on the kind of youthful idler of whom cities across Europe were becoming full at that time — a phenomenon which has led Marilyn Butler and others to suggest that they represented the unproductive intelligentsia from whose ranks future revolutionaries would be drawn. But Mr Swiveller is no revolutionary in the making, though he is certainly contemptuous of the law and eventually a benevolent protector of the poor and vulnerable. When he is found work as a law clerk by the demon dwarf, Quilp, Dick at once settles in to his place of occupation — the brother and sister Sampson and Sally Brass — by getting upon his stool and trying "caricatures of Miss Brass with a pen and ink, whistling very cheerfully all the time." (Chapter 34.)

Whistling here must surely indicate a resolute assertion and keeping up of good cheer. Kent, Antony, and Dick Swiveller whistle for their own entertainment. In doing so, they express a kind of untouchable self-resource. This is therefore different from whistling in the dark, from whistling to keep your courage up. For that supposes or takes for granted a listener. Whistling on such terms may seem strange. Wouldn't silence be preferable? But whistling is a mark of dauntlessness. The enemy may be out there, in which case let them take note that you don't care. You are indifferent to the menace they pose.

Naturally, such indifference can itself be a pose. As the song has it, "Whenever I feel alone,/I hold myself erect,/I whistle a happy tune/So no one will suspect/I'm afraid." Kent is certainly ready to show himself indifferent to all those ranged against Lear, including Lear himself. Whether in disguise or not, Kent's manner of speech is always dauntless. It is, as the O.E.D., defines the word, "bold, intrepid, persevering." Not swaggering but certainly uncowed. No wonder he is a whistler. He whistles to while away the hours, but he also whistles in the face of adversity. His whistling signifies a refusal to submit, whatever the odds, to human enemy or natural force. Such whistling means to be heard. Indeed, without the assumption that it *is* being heard — or overheard — it has no meaning.

This is very like Mark Tapley's whistling. Not long after Mark and young Martin Chuzzlewit have arrived in America, Martin discovers his friend entertaining a "grey-haired black man" by whistling "Rule Britannia," though he stops "the tune at that point where Britons generally are supposed to declare (when it is whistled) that they are never, never, never." (Chapter 17.) In Phiz's illustration of the scene, the black man stares enthralled at Mark, who reclines at ease on a sea-faring trunk, top-hat canted over his brow, propped on an elbow as he whistles and stares unconcernedly back. It's a lovely, comic, but also complex image. It establishes Mark as a man not to be put upon, taking for granted his status as free-born Englishman and implying, by contrast, that the land of the free takes slavery for granted. Whistling as self-expression here is a token of independent selfhood. But then Mark's stopping short of his whistling also implies that at some level he is aware of ways in which, for all that Englishmen take pride in never being slaves, their freedom may be circumscribed, by inner as well as outer fetters: mind-forged manacles (selfishness, hypocrisy, vanity, those major concerns of the novel) as much as criminality and the unjust laws of the state.

Mark Twain's *Autobiography* provides a telling reverse image of such whistling. Here, Twain recalls a moment in his childhood when the deep meaning of someone's whistling was borne in on him.

We had a little slave boy whom we had hired from someone ... he had been brought away from his family and friends, half way across the American continent and sold. He was a cheery spirit, innocent and gentle, and the noisiest creature that ever was, perhaps .... All day long he was singing, whistling, whooping, laughing, — it was maddening, devastating, unendurable. At last I lost my temper and went raging to my mother, and said ... would she please shut him up.

His mother's reply must have sown the seeds of Twain's great novel, *Huckleberry Finn*..

"Poor thing, when he sings, it shows that he is not remembering, and comforts me; but when he is still, I am afraid he is thinking and I cannot bear it. He will never see his mother again; if he can sing, I must not hinder it, but be thankful for it. If you were older, you would understand me; then this friendless child's noise would make you glad."

Whether or no Twain's mother was right in her interpretation of the slave's "noise", she obviously sees in his whistling and singing an expression of unselfconscious happiness — of temporary forgetfulness of his slavery — that assuages her own sense of guilt.

A somewhat related kind of whistling occurs in *Bleak House*. George Rouncewell, former soldier now employed in a London shooting gallery, harbours uneasy thoughts about the northern home he left when setting out for a life of soldiering. "I am such a vagabond still," he thinks, "that I couldn't hold to the gallery a month together, if it was a regular pursuit, or if I didn't camp there, gipsy fashion. Come! I disgrace nobody, and cumber nobody; that's something. I have not done that for many a long year." And so, we are told, "he whistles it off, and marches on." He reacts similarly

Mr. Tapley Succeeds in Finding a Jolly Subject for Contemplation.

when, a little later, having failed to gain entrance to the chambers of the lawyer, Tulkingorn, "this so intensifies his dudgeon, that for five minutes he is in an ill-humour. But he whistles that off, like the rest of it; and marches home to the Shooting Gallery." (Chapter 27.)

Whistling off black thoughts, whistling away your cares, is the physiological expression of psychological release. Henri Matisse told one interviewer that "I'm rather inclined to depression and sometimes see everything in black .... The biggest worry is losing my love of work. I can put up with the blackest despair by whistling or singing." Such whistling isn't an expression of careless rapture but it does demonstrate an assertion of freedom, a snapping of the mind-forged manacles of emotional moods — to put it no more strongly — that threaten mental well-being. In this respect, Rouncewell's fictional progenitor may be the "Whistler" in Walter Scott's *Heart of Midlothian,* a man whose extraordinary story includes his being the lost (foundling) son of an evil ex-smuggler who through various nefarious means becomes a Lord, leaving his son more or less literally to go native. By the end of the novel, the whistler, having been transported into slavery in America, escapes and takes up with native Amerindians. Whistling is here not merely defiant, it is an assertion of identity, a kind of self-engineered proof of manumission. Jeannie Deans, the heroine of Scott's novel, is told by the youth, who is described as "a tall, lathy, young savage ... his gesture free and noble," that "I have no other name than the whistler."

Whistling can also be an expression of delight, of absorption in making music, of rapture, even. In chapter 17 of *The Catcher in the Rye,* Holden Caulfield recalls an acquaintance called Harris Macklin. Macklin is a bore with a raspy voice that gets on Holden's nerves because he talks so much. But all is not lost. "The sonuvabitch," Holden admits,

> could whistle better than anybody I ever heard. He'd be making his bed, or hanging up stuff in the closet — he was always hanging up stuff in the closet — it drove me crazy —

and he'd be whistling while he did it .... He could even whistle classical stuff, but most of the time he just whistled jazz. He could take something very jazzy, like 'Tin Roof Blues', and whistle it so nice and easy — right while he was hanging stuff up in the closet — that it would kill you."

Holden doesn't tell Macklin that he admires his whistling — "I mean you don't just go up to someone and say 'You're a terrific whistler,'" but the whistling gives him pause. "So I don't know about bores. Maybe you shouldn't feel too sorry if you see some swell girl getting married to them. They don't hurt anybody most of them, and maybe they're secretly all terrific whistlers or something." Macklin's whistling is unlike Stradlater's. It suggests a genuine depth of feeling for music, even a sensitivity — not that Holden would use such a word — that marks him out as potentially a more considerate lover than Stradlater will ever be.

Holden's genuine delight in Macklin's whistling is over-matched in the appreciation shown by the protagonist of Nicholson Baker's *The Mezzanine*, when he hears, coming from the men's room,

the roar of a flushed urinal, followed by 'I'm A Yankee Doodle Dandy,' whistled with infectious cheerfulness and lots of rococo tricks — most notably the difficulty yodel-trill technique, used on the 'ee' of the 'dandy' in which the whistler gets his lips to flip the sound binarily between the bass tone and a higher pitch that is I think somewhere between a major third and a perfect fourth above it (why it is not a true harmonic but rather perceptibly out of tune has puzzled me often — something to do with the physics of pursed lips?): a display of virtuosity forgivable only in the men's room, and not, as some salesmen seem to think, in the relative silence of working areas, hate exuding from the suspended razor points, as the whistler passed.

Tunes sometimes lived all day in the men's room, sustained by successive users, or remembered by a previous user as he re-entered the tiled liveliness of the room. Once, hopped-up after several cups of coffee, I loudly whistled the bouncy opening of the tune that starts out 'All I Want is a Room Somewhere,' and then stopped, embarrassed, because I realised that I had interrupted someone else's quieter and more masterly whistling of a soft rock standard with my toneless, aerated tweets; later that day, though, I heard a stylishly embellished version of my tune whistled at the copying machine by someone who must have been in the stalls during my roughshod interruption of the soft rocker.

Whistler and listener are together and yet apart in this deftly attentive, comic but entirely serious set of observations.

III

This has a bearing on, and in a sense is expressed in, Franz Kafka's almost impossibly rich, teasing late story, "Josefine, the Singer, or the Mouse People", mentioned earlier. The story is far too complex to be smoothed out in the few paragraphs that follow, though it seems proper to say that it is, in part at least, a wonderfully sly meditation on the nature of art, including the consideration of whether there's any such thing. We might have discussed the story in the chapter on "Whistling as Communication," it could have found a place in the chapter on "Whistling as Entertainment," but we choose to include it here because Josefine's sounds are undoubtedly a form of self-expression. They express her identity, or so she claims. They reveal her to be an artist.

Or do they? The question goes to the very marrow of the story. What *are* the sounds she makes? How shall they be described? Does Josefine sing or does she merely whistle? She has no doubt that she sings, is an artist. Those who hear her are inclined to think she whistles, is therefore quite like them, is someone whose sounds they can imitate. But even this is at issue. Because, in accepting her own self-evaluation as someone apart from them, they also think that she is inimitable. How come, then, that it seems possible to imitate what she does? The fact that these questions can't be resolved is essential to the story's teasing, enigmatic, comedic nature. If the sounds Josefine makes belong to song then she is indeed special. But it may be that she does no more — or of course less — than whistle. Early on in the story, the unnamed protagonist reflects that "we have at least an intimation of what song is, and Josefine's art does not really accord with it. Can it be described as song at all? Might it not just be a form of whistling? And whistling is something with which we are all familiar, whistling is the true aptitude of our people, or perhaps not an aptitude so much as the characteristic expression of our lives." This quotation, we need to explain, comes from the Penguin edition of *Kafka: Metamorphosis & Other Stories,* translated by Michael Hofmann, and does not appear in most rival versions. This is because other translators, aware that the German for "to whistle" is pfeifen, use the word "piping." But Hofmann's "whistling" makes far better sense, in an English context at least. Whistling, not piping, is what we all do.

In Kafka's story, "we" are the Mouse People. As such "we" wouldn't dare to consider the musical sounds "we" make as having the nature of true art. Certainly, Josefine insists on an absolute distinction between the sounds she utters and those of her many imitators, even if they sometimes dare to think that the sounds are identical. Hence, the following. "We admire in her what we are far from admiring in ourselves," the Mouse Person narrator says, and he goes on:

> She is in full agreement with us. I was present once when someone, as must happen all the time, referred her to the general popular art of whistling, only very discreetly, but

70

even that was too much for Josefine. I have yet to see a smile on anyone as pert and as conceited as the one she put on then; she, who to look at is the embodiment of delicacy ... looked positively shrewish; she may even have sensed as much herself in her great sensitivity, because she quickly mastered herself. At any rate, she denies any connection between her art and whistling.

Yet "There was one occasion when some naughty little thing started innocently whistling during Josefine's singing. Well, it was no different from what we were hearing from Josefine herself ... and yet we quelled the disturbance with angry hisses and whistles ..." Josefine is angry, but also resigned: "it is after all her opinion that she is singing to a lot of deaf ears; there is a lot of applause and enthusiasm, but real insight, she claims, she has long since learnt to do without."

A little later, the narrator admits that "as whistling is one of our unthinking habits," so, because Josefine's art cheers people up and "we" whistle when we are cheerful, it might be expected that "such whistling carries on in Josefine's auditorium." But no. Her listeners do not whistle, "rather they are as quiet as mice." Art requires a reverence that rules out a whole-hearted, enthusiastic response, and this, though the listeners can't tell the difference between what Josefine insists is her "art", and ordinary, unremarkable whistling, and even though the narrator at one point admits that the artist in fact has a "feeble little voice."

Not only this. There are moments when those who claim to be enraptured by Josefine's art nevertheless claim that "She can't even whistle; that's how hard she has to try to produce not song — we're not talking about song here — but just a passable version of bog-standard whistling."

What it *may* come down to is this. "Whistling is the language of our people, only there are some who whistle all their lives and never know it, but here [where Josefine performs] the whistling is detached from the fetters of everyday life, and it frees us too for a little while. We wouldn't miss these performances for the world." Art is solace against everyday life and its cares. But art is made out of the everyday, and art, for all its granted *cachet* of unique distinction, may therefore be no better than or distinguishable from the everyday. We can all whistle. Perhaps, then, we are all artists, though Kafka's great, teasing story isn't going to tell us, the mouse people, one way or the other. That's for us to decide. And while we are trying to do that, Josefine will go on smiling shrewishly and claiming her natural right to be considered as someone apart, not a whistler at all, even if that's what she sounds like to us. Whistling, the music of the people, is not art.

IV

Josefine knows what effect she produces, or wishes to produce, on those who crowd into the auditorium where she performs. She is after all a self-conscious artist. But what of the effect whistling can have on the unintended, unsuspecting hearer? Consider, for example, Sarah Orne Jewett's story, "A White Heron." This is about a young girl who lives with her aunt in a deep wood in Maine. Her loneliness is intruded upon by a young man to whom she is at first deeply attracted. But her attitude changes to apprehension, then panic, when she discovers that for a living he shoots birds whose carcasses he sells to a taxidermist. She knows, but will not reveal, the whereabouts of the nest of a white heron for which the man is searching. In the end he gives up and leaves. The tale is not so much an allegory as a fable of awakening sexuality, of its allurements and of the girl's fears. It is very discreetly managed and never more so than at the close, when Jewett writes of how "many a night", the girl, grieving over the man's disappearance, "heard the echo of his whistle haunting the pasture path as she came home ..."

The sexual glamour of such whistling is inextricably bound up with danger. "She forgot even her sorrow at the sharp report of his gun and the piteous sight of thrushes and sparrows dropping silent to the ground, their songs hushed and their pretty feathers stained and wet with blood." John Bunyan, it is worth noting, advises birds in "Upon the Lark and the Fowler", to "Take no heed to the fowler's tempting call,/This whistle he enchanteth birds withal," whistling being a device used to decoy birds into nets or within range of a gun. Unlike Jewett, Bunyan *is* writing allegorically: the fowler is the Devil, luring frail humans to their destruction with seductive music. And who more likely to be seduced than women?

Here, then, it's impossible not to touch on the identification of wandering men, especially Gypsies, with all that lies beyond prudential living, including a sexual vitality, a careless largesse. Whistling in this context can be a way of cocking a snook at respectability, an assertion of the right to song, and be damned with you. "He whistled and sang, till the green wood rang,/And he won the heart of a lady." These words sum up, decorously it must be said, what we might think of as the orientalising of wandering travellers. Wanderers are not to be compared to people who have somewhere to get to, have an end in view. They are guided by their own will, they are not at someone else's beck and call.

Edward Thomas's envy of the imagined life of the wanderer prompts several of his finest poems, though such envy is by no means always for an imagined sexual freedom. Among the poems of especial relevance is "An Old Song."

I was not apprenticed nor ever dwelt in famous Lincolnshire;
I've served one master ill and well much more than seven year;
And never took up poaching as you shall quickly find;
But 'tis my delight of a shiny night in the season of the year.

I roamed where nobody had a right but keepers and squires, and there
I sought for nests, wild flowers, oak sticks, and moles, both far and near,
And had to run from farmers, and learnt the Lincolnshire song:
'Oh, 'tis my delight of a shiny night in the season of the year.' ...

73

Since then I've thrown away a chance to fight a gamekeeper;
And I less often trespass, and what I see or hear
Is mostly from the road or path by day: yet still I sing
'Oh, 'tis my delight on a shiny night in the season of the year.'

For if I am contented, at home or anywhere,
Or if I sigh for I know not what, or my heart beats with some fear,
It is a strange kind of delight to sing or whistle just:
'Oh, 'tis my delight of a shiny night in the season of the year.'

And with this melody on my lips and no one by to care,
Indoors, or out on shiny nights or dark in open air,
I am for a moment made a man that sings out of his heart:
'Oh, 'tis my delight of a shiny night in the season of the year.'

In her invaluable edition of Thomas's *Collected Poems*, Edna
Longley notes that from his earliest years Thomas was deeply
attracted to folk song, and she quotes his remark that "I prefer any
country church or chapel to Winchester or Chichester or
Canterbury Cathedral, just as I prefer 'All round my hat' or 'Somer
is icumen in', to Beethoven." (*The South Country*, p. 4.) The "strange
kind of delight" Thomas, or the poem's spokesman, takes in choosing
to "sing or whistle just" — that is, to set aside any other kind of
language — is because it answers better than other forms of expression the need to respond to sighs for "I know not what" or to cope
with his heart beating "with some fear." So that even the "tamed"
wanderer, constrained by bourgeois considerations, who turns away
from scrapping with a gamekeeper — as Thomas when out walking
with Frost on one guilt-inducing occasion had done — choosing to
keep to the straight and narrow ("the road or path"), he may nevertheless find himself suddenly released into music that evokes the
freedom he once knew.

Melody, whether sung or whistled, is the most complete utterance of what elsewhere Thomas calls "the quintessence of many

lives and passions .... The words, in league with a fair melody, lend themselves to infinite interpretations, according to the listener's heart." (*The Heart of England*, p. 227.) In this instance, the listener's heart is also that of the singer or whistler, one that contains impulses and fears beyond rational language. Singing out of the heart is impulsive. So is whistling. Like singing, whistling seems to start up almost without our will. We simply find ourselves doing it. Self-expression may be expressiveness, but it is also unselfconscious,. We find ourselves, the heart of ourselves, *in* whistling.

But there is, too, reason which is instinct with a life beyond the ratiocinative. Thomas touches on this in another poem, "The Penny Whistle." Hearing the "nursery melody" which a youth, hidden in a thicket, plays on his tin whistle, is enough to set off in the listener memories of innocence, of a lost and perhaps irrecoverable world. The poem was written in January, 1915, at a time when Thomas was deciding that he must enlist in the war against Germany.

There is no evidence that T.S. Eliot had the line quoted above in mind when he came to write *Burnt Norton*. But can it be mere coincidence that he was editor at Faber when in 1936 the firm took over responsibility for publishing Thomas's first *Collected Poems*, which is precisely the time Eliot was beginning to work on his own poem? At the very least, it feels proper to compare Thomas's boy hiding apart in the thicket with the moment where Eliot writes of how "the bird called, in response to/The unheard music hidden in the shrubbery," although in *Burnt Norton* the bird calls "Go... for the leaves were full of children,/Hidden excitedly containing laughter," whereas laughter may not be what is evoked by the boy's tune in "The Penny Whistle."

It is, however, present in "The Gypsy," where Thomas allows himself to be conned out of a pipeful of tobacco by a Gypsy girl who had asked for money, although "with that much victory she laughed content," while her brother drums the tambourine, stamps his feet and plays on the mouth-organ "a rascally Bacchanal dance/Over the hills and far away." As with the old song of

"Lincolnshire Poacher," this music summons up a freedom remote from those class constraints of pre-1914 England against which Thomas chafed and which, *mutatis mutandis,* are also present in the Prufrockian bondage of those who can never risk the awful daring of a moment's surrender, or who, in Forster's terms, turn their backs on a room with view. No dancing over the hills for *them.* And though it takes a good deal of invention to hear in the Gypsy boy's music "an occasion of drunken revelry; an orgy," which is how the O.E.D. defines bacchanal, there is in Thomas's poem a real yearning for the freedom of the "rascally" dance, even though (or should that be because) the O.E.D. glosses "rascally" as "Unprincipled or dishonest", as well as "Belonging to the rabble or the lowest social class."

Besides, the actual song, "Over the hills and far away" is one of such lovely, lilting exuberance that it seems made for dancing, just as the words going with the tune imply a land of Cockaigne, of uninhibited generosities. Oddly enough, "Over the Hills" is the title of another Thomas poem. Oddly, for sure, if you agree with most commentators, including Longley, that the title is doubtful. There is apparently no reliable evidence that Thomas so named a poem which, Longley says, is about remembering remembering, and doesn't feature hills. The title is, so she asserts, at best "questionable".

But is it? The key moment is surely when Thomas recalls the day he passed

> To a new country, the path I had to find
> By half-gaps that were stiles once in the hedge,
> The pack of scarlet clouds running across
> The harvest evening that seemed endless then
> And after, and the inn where all were kind,
> All were strangers. I did not know my loss
> Till one day twelve months later suddenly
> I leant upon my spade and saw it all,
> Though far beyond the sky-line.

The poem's title seems perfectly to fit this. For what Thomas tries to recall isn't so much a real as an *imagined* place, one where of a harvest evening "all were kind/All were strangers." Fullness, contented fellowship that at the time seemed lasting.

"Over the hills and far away": song (and whistling) can release a vision of and yearning for the great good place, one that is always beyond the grasp of present reason. Edwardian England was a period uniquely steeped in such yearning, although it survives into later times, at least as a kind of romantic after-echo. It is evident in the appeal of "The Gypsy Rover," written by Leo McGuire in Dublin in 1950, and one of the most performed and recorded of all modern folk songs.

> He is no gypsy my father she said
> But lord of these lands over
> And I will stay till my dying day
> With my whistling gypsy rover.

The Gypsy rover, free to roam where he will, like Lob, is a "natural" lord of the land. "I kept my spirit with the free," Clare says at the end of his intense lyric "A Vision," and for him the Gypsy is an embodiment of the freedom of the land, of the wanderer unconstrained by acts of enclosure, whether legal or social. And behind Clare is Robert Burns, who in his first "Epistle to J. Lapraik," famously discomforts those "Critic-folk", who cock their noses at the "unlettered" daring to make a song, by his unfailingly adroit act of verse-making, one which not merely asserts but proves his skill as a "makir":

> Gie me a spark o' Nature's fire,
> That's a' the learning I desire;
> Then, tho' I drudge thro' dub an' mire
> At pleugh or cart,

My Muse, tho' hamely in attire,
May touch the heart

Burns signs off by asking Lapraik to send "twa lines" to him, "who am,/most fervent,/While I can either sing, or whissle,/Your friend and servant."

V

In the poems considered above, the nature of individual self-expression is inferred by the auditor. This is however helped or, it may be, hindered, by assumptions that routinely (and no doubt unquestioningly) link whistler with occupation. Rogues are merry whistlers. Gypsy whistling signals freedom from convention. Ploughmen — especially — and other agricultural workers whistle about their tasks "thoughtlessly". This epithet usefully combines the meanings of "mental vacancy" and "without care." In Samuel Johnson's references to Milton and Gay, whistling is identified not merely with the whistler's work but with what might be called a kind of personality. "The ploughman leaves the talk of day,/And trudging homeward whistles on the way." Does Gay mean to indicate that such whistling reveals the ploughman as stoic, inured to hardship, or happy to be released from labour? Either way, whistling is to be expected of the ploughman. He does it as naturally as he trudges. (Or, in Gray's variations, "plods".) It's as though he doesn't choose the work but that the work chooses him.

Moreover, in this as in other rural occupations, whistling goes with isolation. You don't, it seems, whistle in company. Or perhaps it's more accurate to say that you don't need to whistle in company. Whistling keeps you company. It *is* your company. O. Henry's Whistling Dick, the wandering hobo, needs no company other than his whistling. And yet such whistling is held not so much to mark individuality as a type. Whistling, every bit as much as dress and speech patterns, is taken to be a social marker. There is, it seems therefore safe to say, a gap, often a wide one, between what prompts someone to whistle and how that whistling is interpreted. A rogue may not, after all, be merry, a Gypsy may be forlorn, a ploughman may have many cares. Not all the tunes that are whistled are happy ones.

VI

And yet certain whistlers are — or at least were — the carriers of a boisterous energy which seemed expressive of their trade. To return once more to errand-boys of the kind whom it was once common to see speeding about town on their heavy-laden front-panniered bicycles, they were surely the epitome of cheerful assertiveness? No doubt the bicycles themselves seemed a marvellous empower-ment — true joy-riding — for youths whose intrepid manner of weaving in and out of traffic, mounting pavements at speed and coming to sudden halts, often in front of startled pedestrians, made them seem a cross between cavalrymen at the charge, point-to-point racers and those wild west heroes of Saturday-morning cinema: Hoot Gibson, Tom Mix, Roy Rogers, Gene Autry, others. Packs of Rizla roll-your-own cigarette papers used to show a cowboy roping a steer with one hand while, with the other, he rolled himself a cigarette. Such sprezzatura! Just so, errand boys would steer one-handed through the busiest streets, their panniers laden with joints of meat or piled high with greengrocery, spare hand — the gun-hand? — dandled loosely at their sides. A key element in this display of exuberant panache was their whistling, loud, insis-tent, and not usually of a recognisable tune, more a way of insisting "Here I am, for this I came."

Can group whistling be a form of self-expression? This is marginal territory. There is a moment in John Buchan's *The Thirty-Nine Steps* when the protagonist, Richard Hannay, needing to disguise himself as a milkman, gets away with it not merely by imitating the milkman's "jaunty swing," but by "whistling gaily."

Later, however, tramping the Scottish highlands, Hannay pauses by a stream: "Somehow the place soothed me and put me at my ease. I fell to whistling as I looked into the green depths, and the tune which came to my lips was 'Annie Laurie.'" Hannay's whistling attracts the attention of another fisherman, "and as he neared me he too began to whistle. The tune was infectious, for he followed my suit."

Whistling as a form of hostile comment, the equivalent of jeering or booing, varies from the derisive to the downright condemnatory. Whistling at referees, at bad theatrical performance, at unpopular public speakers, is both instinctive and organised. One person starts and others join in. Or don't, as the mood takes them. And this presumably is significant. If the whistling doesn't command assent it will die an early death. It isn't melodic, this whistling, it's more like "rough music", the music of the skimmington, the antithesis of all that's meant by harmony and concord. It is or at least can also be liberating, a way of asserting a common response, one of rejection, to despised authority. "Take but degree away .... and hark what discord follows." Perhaps such whistling is best thought of as an expression of *demos*, a deliberate noising of displeasure at degree. Less excusably, it can be a form of bullying, even a confirmation of degree. At all events, Dickens refers to the practice of "whistling down on Wednesday nights" (*The Old Curiosity Shop*, Chapter 38) which was apparently the method sitting MPs used in order to see off private members' bills, especially, so Dickens says, any intended for the general good: "the people's health and comforts."

VII

John Clare is the English poet who above all others devotes attention to whistling and whistlers. Given his origins and place of birth, this isn't perhaps surprising. As Ronald Blythe notes, Clare's native Northamptonshire was "like every county filled with noisy labouring children ... loud with their singing and shouting, their

80

whistling and general hubbub." (*At Helpston*, Black Dog Books, 2011.) But it took a remarkable poet not merely to report the amount of whistling among his fellow countrymen but to understand and register its significance. Other poets writing about rural life inevitably mention whistling, but Clare knows it to be intrinsic to agricultural work and leisure. *The Shepherd's Calendar* (1827) provides remarkable testimony to the attention Clare pays to whistling, both as collective and individual forms of musical expression, ones which run the gamut from joy to stoical acceptance.

As already mentioned, there is an important precedent to Clare's work in Bloomfield's *Farmer's Boy*, which reports the singing and whistling of rural workers, mingled with animal noises in what Bloomfield calls a "strange concert." No doubt encouraged by the example of the poet he praised as the English Theocritus, Clare draws attention to, as well as pleasure from, the charivari of sounds he heard all about him at Helpston and elsewhere. He was attuned to them. The result, both in *The Shepherd's Calendar*, and more generally in his work, is a uniquely detailed and loving account of whistling.

Country boys habitually announce themselves through whistling. Such whistling is a kind of piping down the valleys, wild, exuberant, unrestrained. Not untrained, though. Boys, however young, are learning to whistle as their elders do, imitating their songs, their whistled commands, the raucous two-fingered call to sheep and cattle, the rasping sound made by blowing against a blade of grass pressed between thumbs that are held vertically against the lips.

All this activity produces a music which is redolent of place. In "Pastoral Poesy," Clare remarks that such poetry "sings and whistles in [the rural poet's]mind,/And then it talks aloud." Clare loved traditional tunes and collected over a hundred which he set down — "scratted" — using a notation system he could then play on the violin and, of course, whistle. This was a common enough practice among country musicians, for many of whom a tune was one they inherited from previous generations and which they themselves were liable to adapt or modify as talent or the fancy took them. Variations are part of this tradition and each place is identified with particular sets of such variations.

In "The Shepherd's Hut," Clare goes much further in identifying how place and music are braided together. "Those rude old tales," he says, meaning tales that were sung as well as spoken, "mans memory augurs ill/Thus to forget the fragments of old days/These long old songs ..." The songs were recalled and endlessly sung by shepherds, "Rude chroniclers of ancient minstrelsy," who "Left their old music like a summer bee/For summers breeze to murmuer oer and die/& in these ancient spots — mind and eye/Turn listeners." The mind's eye and ear combine to summon up a peopled history, one known familiarly through song, melody, cadence.

Whistling inevitably has its part to play because, in *The Shepherd's Calendar* as in so much of his poetry, Clare is the historian of a place irrecoverably altered by all that is implied by enclosure. The past is out of reach, yet at the same time so vividly present that in writing about it he instinctively, or so it must seem, uses the present tense. Hence, for example, "The driving boy beside his team" who will "oft burst loud in fits of song/And whistles as he reels along" ("May", *The Shepherd's Calendar*); or the "Horseboy" who "Whistling and bawling loud and long," whistles the louder as "eve grows long"; or the ploughmen who "go whistling to their toils" ("February" — *The Shepherd's Calendar*); or the shepherd himself who "With whistle, barking dogs and chiding scold/[Will drive] the bleating sheep from fallow fold." What in "July" Clare calls "the busy noise of man and brute," and in "August," where, writing about summer activities of all kinds, he tells us the fields are "alive with sultry noise," he later, in his asylum days, recalls in the following lines:

Joy then was up and whistled by
A merry tune which I had known full long

But could not to my memory wake it back
Until the ploughman changed it to the song
Of happiness, how simple is thy tack.
("Ploughman Singing")

To repeat: not all this whistling was joyous. Some was purely functional, some provided a way of anaesthetising the boredom of routine. Joy, though, is not to be discounted.

VIII

And, finally in this chapter, we must mention how whistling can indulge fantasies, release imagination, be a way not so much of piping down the wild as piping it up. You whistle up your dreams, become transported by them, give yourself over to the music, safe in the knowledge that nobody can share your dream, that you're free to let the tunes you whistle take you wherever you will. An example of this occurs in W.G. Sebald's *The Emigrants*, when the narrator remembers one of the characters, Paul, who

> was in the habit of whistling continuously as he walked across the fields. He was an amazingly good whistler: the sound he produced was marvellously rich, exactly like a flute's. And even when he was climbing a mountain he would with apparent ease whistle whole runs and ties in connected sequence, not just anything, but fine, thoroughly composed passages and melodies that none of us had ever heard before, and which gave a wrench to my heart whenever, years later, I rediscovered them in a Bellini opera or Brahms sonata.

And here is John Hartley Williams' poem, "Music While You Walk."

I'm just a natural whistler, one of those
Lip symphonisers, fifeing
An Indian and his maiden down wild white water
With this off-key instrument of mine
I tootle sullen urban streets
Into deep romantic chasms.

On a mirror lagoon, they drift, becalmed
I need a melody for the floor of a canoe
Oo la la. Such modulations. It's stupendous
How deeply tongue can moisten flutehole
As I make the diddly stops against
The onward rush of sexually lonely air
Piping imaginary blades of grass between my thumbs
Almost a great tune rising from the breaks

A funny, melancholy-exuberant, self-aware poem which, in its
over-the-top fantasies of sexual longing, delights in the mind's
ability to whistle up Hollywood dream worlds from the urban
streets the "natural whistler" patrols.

Whistling as Communication

I

The simplest form of whistling as a means of communication is one
long blast. Policeman use mechanical whistles to direct traffic. In
ball games, referees blow them to signal the start of play or to bring
it to a halt. Time was, schoolteachers would use a whistle to bring
classes to order. And in the absence of mechanical whistles fingers
had to do. To make a wolf whistle, as this form of whistling is usually
called, you push the first two fingers of each hand under your
rolled-up tongue and then, in the words of one adept wolf-whistler,
poet and publisher Jenny Swann, "blow like hell." She learned this
form of whistling as a teenager, determined, she says, that in this
respect at least, anything boys could do she would do as well. But it
seems that among women teachers at elementary schools such
whistling was, if not common, then by no means unknown. Women
teachers may not be able to out-bellow their male counterparts, but
they can whistle as powerfully.

According to the O.E.D., however, a wolf-whistle is not so much a
single blast used to back-up the authority of the whistler as one
"esp. one by a man, expressing sexual admiration or attraction." But
this is to identify the whistle with the two note sound, the second a
downward glissando, especially associated with "scaffolding ... and
workmen whistling." The wolf-whistle as an indicator of sexual
approval has now largely disappeared, almost certainly because it
is no longer socially acceptable, a matter which may well owe less

to male sensitivity than the increasingly derisive responses of women targeted. One such response, "my teddy bear's got a bigger whistle than that," gained a good deal of currency among women students at midland universities in the early 1980s.

Whether expressing sexual attraction or calling an unruly class to order or being used to attract someone's attention, the wolf-whistle is very different from the dog-whistle. This mechanical aid, rather like a pipistrelle squeak, reaches notes too high for the human ear to register. Hence, the adoption of the term "dog-whistle" to the particularly nasty campaign pre-election by the Conservative party when Michael Howard was its leader, and anti-immigration, not to say racist, policies were silently endorsed. In this campaign, steered by an Australian, Lynton Crosby, who had experienced success with it in winning successive elections for Brian Howard's right-of-centre party in Australia, nothing was said. Everything was implied. A similar dog-whistle element was present in the same party's poster advertisements in the 1980s, which simply showed a bulldog with a Union Jack collar tag. Crosby is now back advising the current prime-minister, David Cameron. His dirty tricks are a world away from Toodle's admonishing his children not to "play secret games. Keep your whistles going, and let's be hearing from you."

They are also a world away from the shepherd who communicates with his dog by whistling instructions in how to work the sheep. Such whistling is necessarily open. There are essentially four different whistled sounds by which the shepherd communicates orders to his dog. "Walk on" — for the dog in position behind the sheep — consists of three short blasts. "Come by" — go left — two blasts; "away" — go right — is signified by a long note rising toward the end. "Lie down" is a similar note but this time with a swooping downward glissando. Steven Neeston, who trains border collies from his home in rural Leicestershire, and from whom this information comes, began life in Co. Donegal, and after leaving the Inniskilling Fusiliers, where his prowess as a piper was put to good use, tended cattle before becoming a shepherd. In his early days as shepherd Neeston whistled by mouth, then adopted a titanium whistle until one icy morning the whistle literally froze on his lips and he had to soak them in scalding hot water in order to release the metal; he now uses a plastic whistle, shaped like a miniature purse with a flat top, an inch in length at its widest, and flanged to form two curved lips that are about an eighth of an inch apart. Through this whistle, he can blow not only his commands to the dogs he trains, but also tunes, traditional Irish melodies among them.

Such tunes could doubtless once be heard coming from fields and hillsides some distance off. They and the more functional shepherds' whistling once gladdened the morning air, and came not merely from hill shepherds but all agricultural workers who needed to communicate with the animals, especially dogs and horses, on which they relied. In this context it probably isn't possible to distinguish whistling as communication from whistling as self-communing, because they must on occasions shade into one another, just as Edward Lear's butcher boy was almost certainly whistling for the hell of it at the same time as alerting householders to his approach. And even the most functional of whistling can be managed with style and individual flourish.

II

This points to a connection between birdsong and human whistling. Both forms of whistling can be, while self-expressive, also functional. But despite the assertions of some sentimentalists, this is about as far as it goes. A male bird sings or whistles in order to mark out his territory and to announce his presence to a female of the species. His whistling may be imitated by a listening human, just as — or so the testimony of Ian Clayton's friend suggests — the bird may itself learn to imitate human whistling. This doesn't, however, imply meaningful communication between bird and man. When Dick Fagin was learning to whistle like a blackbird, so he thought, it was because "Whistling was a way of identifying yourself across distances, especially at night, with other men working for the same company. Very useful. Getting it right was a work of art though." *(Men of the Tideway.)* It is, of course, entirely possible that the blackbird Fagin heard whistling the same signal as the lighter-men he worked with was imitating the men's whistling signal.

Italo Calvino's short story "The Blackbird's Whistle" takes a sardonic view of its protagonist, Mr Palomar, who considers the whistling of a blackbird "identical with a human whistle," even though it represents "the efforts of someone not terribly skilled at whistling." This prompts Palomar to speculate that "if a man were to invest in whistling everything he normally invests in words, and if the blackbird were to modulate into his whistling all the unspoken truth of his natural condition, then the first step would have been taken toward bridging the gap between what and what? Nature and culture. Silence and speech."

"A blackbird unskilled at whistling." Leave aside the question of the adequacy of Palomar's hearing, or Calvino's ironic reflection on that, the point, as he well knows and certainly intends, is that attempts to bridge the gap between nature and culture usually produce the kind of anthropomorphism which Ruskin called the pathetic fallacy. Lawrence had great fun exposing this fallacy in his account of Keats's "Ode to the Nightingale." In his little essay, "The Nightingale", D.H. Lawrence playfully dismantles the poet's claims for the bird's song and all that Keats takes from it. "Still wouldst thou sing," the poet mourns, "and I have ears in vain, —/To thy high requiem become a sod."

Get away, is Lawrence's amused, sardonic response.

How astonished the nightingale would be if he could be made to realise what sort of answer the poet was answering to his song. He would fall off the bough with amazement. Because a nightingale, when you answer him back, only shouts and sings louder. ... Suppose you, a mere mortal, happen to be sitting on the shady bank having an altercation with the mistress of your heart, hammer and tongs, then the chief nightingale swells and goes at it like Caruso in the Third Act — simply a bursting frenzy of music, singing you down, till you simply can't hear yourself speak to quarrel ....

Adieu! Adieu! Thy plaintive anthem fades ....

It never was a plaintive anthem — it was Caruso at his jauntiest. But don't try to argue with a poet.

To be fair to Keats, he wasn't claiming to answer the bird. He'd imagined himself as falling silent. Dead, in fact, having ceased upon the midnight with no pain. But don't try to argue with a critic — not, anyway, a critic as wonderful as Lawrence is.

What, though, would Lawrence have made of the little brown bird which appears toward the end of O. Henry's "Whistling Dick," and which is at least momentarily stunned into silence by the hobo's virtuoso performance.

From the path along the levee there burst forth a jubilant, stirring, buoyant, thrilling whistle, loud and keen, and clear as the clearest notes of the piccolo. The soaring sound rippled and trilled and arpeggioed. as the songs of wild birds do not, but it had a wild free grace that, in a way, reminded the small brown bird of something familiar, but what exactly he could not tell. There was in the sound a call, a reveille, that all birds know; but a great waste of lavish unmeaning things that art had added and arranged, and the little brown bird sat with his head on one side until the sound had died away in the distance.

Human whistling is different from the whistling of a bird because it is or anyway can be self-conscious, artful, a point on which Calvino would agree. The bird could have learnt to imitate Whistling Dick's "lavish unmeaning things," as the blackbird in Ian Clayton's anecdote learns to imitate human whistling, but what would be the point? The little brown bird needs his breakfast and so shoots down "like a brown bullet upon a big fat worm that was wriggling along the levee path." Hunger comes before art. To adapt Brecht, Grub (or worm) first, then aesthetics.

Lawrence, though, would want at the very least to suggest that the bird's own soaring sound, while owing nothing to human whistling, has its own "wild, free grace." Where all three writers agree is in accepting and delighting in the otherness of bird-song. If it communicates anything to human ears it is the right to song which Clare claimed for himself and for everything that lives in a creaturely universe. This is the right St Francis of Assisi celebrates in his *Canticle de Creatures*:

> Loué sois-tu, mon Seigneur,
> pour frère Vent,
> et pour l' air et pour les nuages,
> pour l'âzur calme et tous les temps:
> grâce à eux tu maintiens en vie
> toutes les créatures.

III

In the late 1920s, England became gripped by a sensational murder trial. Harry Pace, a quarryman living and working in the Forest of Dean, died in great pain after two weeks of vomiting and diarrhoea, which brought to an end two years of abdominal problems. Although at first his death was attributed to natural causes, the police began to suspect his wife, Beatrice, of poisoning him with arsenic. They arrested her and she was put on trial, charged with having murdered her husband. Her court appearances made headline news, especially when she revealed the romantic nature of their courtship. "In the evenings, as it grew dark," Beatrice told the jury, Harry "would whistle from the wood — two long notes, up and down, and it got so on my mind that at last I went out to him. Even when I had talked to him, he would not go away, but would often spend the night in our pig-sty, so as to be near me. Every night he whistled from the wood and kept on at me to marry him. What was so strange, he hardly said anything, but just telling me to be his wife."

But Harry Pace turned out to be a psychopath. Soon after their marriage, he began to beat his wife, on one occasion so badly that she miscarried. On another occasion he hammered her pet dog to death, on a third he tied her to the bottom of the bed in her nightdress in the cold.

Perhaps not surprisingly the jury found Beatrice innocent of murder, a verdict greeted with wild approval by the vast crowd which had gathered outside the court waiting to greet Beatrice. According to the *Daily Mirror*, when news of the acquittal reached the waiting crowds, "people came running, until the street was choked by thousands of howling men and women." And a correspondent for *The People* reported that "The National Anthem, played by a trumpeter, shrilled above the clamour. In the hush it cause, the judge came out to his carriage, and the crowd rose to him. 'Good old justice!', they bellowed." (John Carter Wood, *The Most Remarkable Woman in England, Poison, celebrity and the trials of Beatrice Pace*, MUP, 2012, p.1.)

This sad tale of domestic brutality and its violent outcome takes its place in a history of whistling because of Beatrice's testimony that her husband-to-be "hardly said anything, but just telling me to be his wife." It's likely that he told her as much by whistling as by speaking. "Every night he whistled from the wood and kept on at me to marry him." Whatever the nature of the man himself, Pace's whistling must have been seductive, full of allure.

Whistle my lad, and I'll come to you. The history of romantic love, of elopements by night, is studded with such references. The maiden confined in a tower or prison-home hears the music of whistling calling her away. Whistling in this context implies a kind of gaiety

91

that exists beyond the limitations of the prudential. As was noted in the previous chapter, Gypsy whistling, the whistling of vagabonds, of rovers, of those who dwell in the green wood, has the lure of a wider, unbounded world. Hence, the song "The Whistling Thief," written by the Irish Samuel Lover (1797-1868) which reports how

There's Pat come over the hill
His darlin' fair to see
Not whistlin' low but shrill
His signal sure to say
If your mother it won't allow
Then come steppin' outside to steal
A kiss behind the barn

The Pied Piper of Hamelin, it's true, plays on a pipe, but that's a kind of mechanical whistle, and when he leads the children away from home what his music promises is

A joyous land,
Joining the town and just at hand,
Where waters gushed and fruit trees grew
And flowers put forth a fairer hue,
And everything was strange and new;
The sparrows were brighter than peacocks here,
And their dogs outran our fallow deer,
And honey-bees had lost their stings,
And horses were born with eagles' wings ...

This is a child's version of Cockaigne, innocent of the sexual allure that goes with the whistling rover who "whistled and sang till the greenwood rang, And he won the heart of a lady." But that said, the magic of a better world elsewhere is communicated in such whistling. Two notes and a whole world is conjured up!

Yet even in the example of Harry Pace it's not so much the whistling itself that has the glamour of allure but what it signifies. The woman he was courting lived in, if not rural poverty, then the limited expectations from which Pace's love might seem to offer an escape. Beatrice, so her daughter, Dorothy, later wrote, "came from plain, working-class people of the Forest of Dean, and a plain, unspoiled woman she has remained." Although her father worked as a gardener, the family was, in Beatrice's own words, "not too poor to have plenty for everybody." Well, possibly. But it also seems that because her parents' increasing difficulties in feeding their children's hungry mouths, Beatrice went into service for three years in London. Dorothy, however, says that "she brought away with her none of the ways of the city. She went to London a country girl and it was a country girl that she returned." *(The Most Remarkable Woman*, p 19.) Difficult not to think that the women are putting what gloss they can on a family beset by rural poverty.

Harry Pace had met Beatrice just before she left for London. "She heard him whistle once, then twice, but took no notice. I didn't know what it meant. No one had ever called me to them on the roads before.'" For Beatrice to say that Harry Pace called to her is as good as to say that he commanded her, much as a shepherd commands his dog or, of course, summons his faithful shepherdess. And indeed her quarryman husband-to-be supplemented his meagre £2 a week pay by keeping a flock of sheep on common land. As though to endorse his worth as shepherd, at the inquest into his death a sheep marked with Pace's initials appeared at the door of the George Inn, Coleford, where the inquest was being held, causing his sister Leah to be taken with a fit of hysterics. "One of his lambs! He loved them all," she cried. It is easy to agree with Tessa Hadley, when in her review of the book for *The Guardian* she comments, "A novelist writing a period piece would struggle to come up with anything so perfect. It's a poignant touch, too," she adds, "that the Pace's isolated home — 'showing signs of extreme poverty' the detective said —

was called Rose Cottage: someone's dream of beauty." (27th November, 2012.)

Here, by way of contrast, we might note that moment in *Sons and Lovers* when Paul Morel unintendedly reveals to Miriam the cooling of his feelings toward her. His whistling gives him away. "One evening as they were walking down by the canal," Lawrence writes, Miriam sensed that "something was troubling him. She knew she had not got him. All the time he whistled softly and persistently. She listened, feeling she could learn more from his whistling than from his speech. It was a sad, dissatisfied tune — a tune that made her feel he would not stay with her." Paul's whistling inadvertently betrays him. Pace, on the other hand, knew exactly what he was up to.

IV

Pace's whistling was one-way communication. At all events, there is no mention of Beatrice ever whistling back to her lover, any more than Miriam whistles. In fact, Miriam rather despises whistling. Having asked Paul why he whistles at all, she wonders why at the very least he doesn't try whistling some Schubert. But in rural life it was by no means unusual for communities, especially those separated by rivers and other natural obstacles, to whistle to each other as a way of keeping in touch and exchanging what might be vital information. Call and response whistling, whether of the kind to be found at the beginning of Joyce's *Ulysses*, or as remembered by Derrick Buttress from his days among the street gangs of his boyhood, are, or anyway were, as basic as they were common.

This whistling was mostly undertaken by men. There are few records of women whistling as a way of communicating with each other or with male companions, though as we shall see below there are exceptions, and women were no doubt told what passed between the male whistlers. They would need to know because the lives of all the community were involved. We are well, how are

The Whistling Boy by Frank Duveneck (1872)

you? Do you expect a good harvest? Are your animals over the worst of the infection you told us about last time we communicated? Will any of you be coming to the next village wedding? Is it true that some of you have seen signs of an enemy approaching? If so, tell us, please.

Whistling in this context — a pattern of long and short notes, rising or falling — was a kind of aural semaphore, or, it might be more accurate to say, Morse Code, though obviously not internationally agreed. It would have been important to ensure that those not intended to hear the messages being exchanged couldn't understand the whistled communication on which they might be eavesdropping ..

Such a means of communication was widespread throughout the ancient world and the practice continued down to modern times. According to some accounts, at least, more than seventy such kinds of whistling between communities are still in existence. There are older villagers in parts of Euboea (Evia), as on other Greek islands, who can reproduce the whistling patterns of their forebears and according to whom genuine whistled conversation, far exceeding conventional greetings, was not merely possible but in regularly use. Within communities, such whistling was passed on from generation to generation. And what is true of the Greek experience is equally true of other parts of the world. Whistling as sophisticated, articulate and *essential* messaging between communities is, or anyway used to be, taken for granted.

Perhaps the prime example is Silbo (Spanish for "whistle"), the whistled language of La Gomera, a small island of the Canary group. This was and to some extent still is, the native language of the Guanches, who inhabited the Canary islands for centuries before the Spanish arrived, and it was first studied in detail by the Linguistician, André Classe, who in a series of articles published throughout the 1950s, explained that the language was not constructed "on prosodic but on purely articulatory features." According to an article in the *National Geographic Magazine* in

2005, which relies for much of its information on Classe and those who followed up his research, shepherds using Silbo "could whistle about relativity theory if they wanted, however they usually talk about other things ... In daily life they use their whistling to communicate short demands, but any Spanish sentence could be whistled."

In a learned article called "Phonetic of the Silbo Gomero" printed in *Archivum Linguisticum, Vol IX, Fasc I,* Classe notes that the whistling is accomplished by the following means.

1. A deep and narrow groove is formed in the tongue-blade which is pushed against the top teeth. 2. One finger obstructs part of the lip aperture. 3. One bent knuckle is inserted between the lips and the tongue-blade rests on it. 4. One finger is inserted into one corner of the mouth and the finger tip rests on the blade. 5. One finger of each hand is inserted into the mouth more or less deeply and they join at the tip of the tongue. 6. The index or the little finger is sharply bent and inserted quite deeply into the mouth. With all these methods except 5 the free hand may be used to form a sort of horn.

See, it's easy.

Silbo, Classe elsewhere explains, is "really a form of speech." And in an article in *The New Scientist,* in 1958, supplies notation for the various vowel and consonantal sounds as well as photographic illustrations showing that this speech was used by both women and men. Given the island's difficult terrain, the fact that it is, in Classe's words, "exceedingly mountainous," and that "deep and narrow gorges" separate communities, whistled messages make perfect sense. And a good whistler ("silbador") can "be heard and understood five miles away or more when conditions are favourable."

Much of the messaging would have been straightforward: enquiries into health, warnings about the weather, exchanges of information about animals. But as they had an intricate speech pattern at their disposal, it is not surprising that silbadors could and did whistle complicated messages to each other. They often chose to whistle rather than speak in a way acceptable to authority. Classe reports that "on Christmas Day, 1862, the Alcalde of San Sebastian (the capital of Gomera) had the doors of the church locked to keep the shepherds out because they persisted in ignoring his injunction not to whistle *the words* of the Psalms during Mass."

Perhaps rivalling the sophistication of Silbo is the whistle speech of the rural community of Sochiapam Chinantec, in the state of Oaxaca, southern Mexico. Here, apparently, all the men can and do use such speech, but not women, although they may understand it. Different whistling styles are used to communicate at different distances. Some whistling is intended for close-up communication, but whistling with fingers in the mouth makes possible communication between men who are more than a mile apart. And there is also a loud falsetto, although this is reserved for circumstances that involve some degree of urgency or as a warning.

Not surprisingly, the whistling between men in close proximity allows for the most intricate form of communication. According to the transcription of a whistled conversation between two men, Marcelino and Francisco, working in adjacent fields, Marcelino is able to ask whether Francisco has planted tangerines among his coffee plants. No, he hasn't. Oranges then? Yes, Francisco has planted oranges. Could he perhaps bring some for his friend? All right, Francisco says, I will if I can. Marcelino presses him. Give me a few of them. Yes, alright, if I'm able to pick them. Francisco seems a tad reluctant to part with any of his oranges, but Marcelino isn't prepared to take the hint. He tells Francisco that he intends to stay working in his own field until evening. He isn't going anywhere, so the two will see each other at close of day, and he will be waiting for the oranges. At which point Francisco gives in. "All right, we'll see each other this evening." And Marcelino, to make sure that the agreement is nailed down, replies "We'll see each other this evening." (For this see the *Summer Institute of Linguistics in Mexico*, 2008.)

Extraordinary, and, as with the inhabitants of Greek island villages and La Gomera, these conversations are carried on by men who, working not far apart from each other, could as easily have used conventional speech in order to communicate. Perhaps there is simply more pleasure to be had from whistling.

Even more extraordinary, perhaps, is the evidence of a language heard until recently in the South of France, at the foot of the Pyrenees. An entry in the "words" section of the magazine, *The Oldie*, for February, 2013, refers to the Irish language journal, *Comhar*, a recent edition of which contained a poem by the poet Ailbhe Ni Ghearbhuigh, translated into English by Billy Ramsell. The poem, at least in the English version, is entitled "Last Blast." It begins

Even now
the people of Aas can remember
the long-ago whistling of the shepherds,
whistles that followed
the acoustic echoey channel
from village to pasture,
whistles that carried the day's tittle-tattle
between herdsmen
and the women of the homesteads,
whistles not understood beyond the limits of their parish.

Ramsell then explains that "When the Nazis invaded/the whistling-tongue kept/Jews from coming to harm", because the shepherds passed "resistance messages" from lip to lip. They even helped crashed Allied pilots reach the border with Spain.

"It hasn't been heard since," the poem concludes:

It has a half-life, this whistling language,
in the memories of certain parishioners
but none now are capable

of producing the sounds.

It was never recorded.

As the note concludes, "Other whistled languages have been found, but none so important as the 'language' of the Aas. What a great pity it is that nobody thought it worthwhile to record its sounds and to note what they meant." This language, now believed to be extinct, is referred to in several accounts of France in the modern period, including Richard Cobb's seminal work, and unsurprisingly those who mention it mourn not only its loss but the fact that nobody thought to take note of how the people of Aas constructed their whistled language before it went for ever.

V

This being so, it is as well to repeat a point made earlier, that a rudimentary form of communication used by the inhabitants of Aas can be found in the whistling of street gangs sending messages to each other over a city's roof tops. "Where are you?" "Here." "Well, we're *here*, so join us as fast as your legs can carry you." Innocent enough, especially if conducted during daylight hours.

But night-time whistling is different.

.... soon the whistling will begin. Young men are calling their girls. Standing down there in the cold, they whistle up at the lighted windows of warm rooms where the beds are already turned down for the night. They want to be let in. Their signals echo down the deep hollow street, lascivious and private and sad. Because of the whistling, I do not care to stay here in the evenings .... Sometimes I determine not to listen to it, pick up a book, try to read. But soon a call is sure to sound, so piercing, so insistent, so despairingly human, that at last I have to get up and peep through the slats of the Venetian blind to make sure that it is not — as I know very well it could not possibly be — for me.

100

So Christopher Isherwood begins the Berlin Diary section of *Goodbye to Berlin*. His account inaugurates what, though Isherwood can't be held responsible for this, soon becomes a cliché: whistling in a dark, lonely street, as indicative of lovelorn melancholy.

But night-time whistling can also suggest something ominous, threatening, or dastardly, though it is unlikely that Homer would have thought any of these terms fit epithets to attach to the doings of Odysseus and Diomedes. In Book 10 of the *Iliad* Homer tells us that the two men volunteer to use the cover of darkness in order to spy on the Trojans and that, as they set off for the enemy, Pallas Athene sends down a heron as a sign of her favour. Although they cannot see the bird, they can hear its crying, "And Odysseus was glad at the bird-sign." They find themselves among the sleeping, exhausted Thracians, who are fighting alongside the Trojan army, and "as a lion advancing on the helpless herds unshepherded of sheep or goats pounces upon them," so Diomedes kills twelve while Odysseus gathers together their horses, intending to take them back to the Greek ships.

Hours later, after much killing and maiming, Odysseus notices that night is fading. The two men now risk discovery. Accordingly, Odysseus "whistled to brilliant Diomedes as a signal to him."

What sound did Odysseus make? Not that of a night heron, for sure. Because *all* types of heron, from the English grey to the American purple, emit what authorities call a kind of croak, and Homer, so his editors agree, specifically uses the word reserved for a high-pitched sound in describing Odysseus's utterence. According to the best authorities, even the night-heron, common in Eastern Europe and perhaps the bird Homer had in mind, makes a noise resembling *quak* or *gowek*, which may be imitable but is scarcely a whistle.

Interestingly, and perhaps instructively, no two of Homer's translators into English can agree on the sound Odysseus makes. Pope looks as though he may be nailing his colours to the mast when he reports that the heron Pallas Athene sends Odysseus and Diomedes is "long-wing'd" (though what heron has short wings?) and that, though the shades obscure the men's view of it, they identify it by its "shrill Clang and whistling Wings." Does Odysseus imitate the sound of the heron's wings, perhaps? Well, no. Pope ducks the crucial matter, because when it comes to the moment of the whistle, he tells us merely that Odysseus "gave his Friend the Signal to retire." Yes, but *what* signal? No whistle is mentioned, not so much as a peep.

Richmond Lattimore, whose version of the *Iliad* is quoted above, is plain and simple. According to him, Odysseus simply whistles, as he does in E.V. Rieu's prose version. But Robert Fagles, in his justly admired translation, and perhaps taking his cue from Pope, makes the wily one give a "shrill whistle." For Robert Fitzgerald, on the other hand, the whistle is "low," whereas Robert Graves in *The Anger of Achilles* has the whistle as sounding "soft."

Admittedly, all this may seem not so much a way of counting angels dancing on a pinhead as trying to work out on which leg they pirouette. Anyway, Homer, who, so recent scholars suggest, was colour-blind — hence the wine-dark sea — could conceivably also have been tone-deaf. On the other hand, whistling at night is bound to alert the suspicions of anyone overhearing it, and Odysseus would hardly have wanted to draw attention to his and Diomedes' presence among the enemy ranks. But that's not to say he whistled either low or soft. He needed Diomedes to hear him. Perhaps, as is suggested below, a shrill whistle was the one most likely to be mistaken for that of a night bird. Perhaps any waking Thracian thought that once you'd heard one night bird you'd heard them all. Or perhaps they went on sleeping.

John Clare reports a telling, daytime, incident of what can happen when whistling is misinterpreted by someone overhearing what was never intended for his ears. Clare was one day accompanied on a walk by a local magistrate, a self-important bigwig eager to be seen in the presence of someone whom John Goodridge and Kelsey Thornton, in their essay, "John Clare: the trespasser," call "the celebrated 'peasant poet.'" According to Clare the magistrate soon began to show off:

> everyone we met gentle or simple he would stop to speak too and almost ask their business nay he woud question those that appeard his inferiors as if they were under going an examination in a court of justice — once when we were going to see Belvoir Castle while walking by a plantation a labourer happend to break out into a brisk loud whistle of a song tune and he instantly stopt to listen and swore they were poachers and bade me go on the other side to watch which way they started I tryd to convince him that the whistle was a song tune but it was no use — and as soon as the fellow heard or perhaps saw that he was suspected tho hid from us I expect he felt fearful and stopt his whistle this convinced the other that his opinion was right — so after watching awhile the fellow made his appearance and met us to know if we was waiting for him He askd him his business there and he said he was putting down fencing which satisfied the magistrate — who I verily believe mistrusted every stranger for thieves and vagabonds.
> (John Clare, *Autobiographical Writings*, p. 123.)

If Clare needed to explain to the magistrate that the whistling they had overheard was in fact a song it must mean that the man of law took what the poet knew to be self-communing, and the "right to song," to be a whistled communication with other "poachers." But as Clare would have been well aware,, you wouldn't whistle to yourself if you were doing something illegal, not unless you were very stupid. You'd keep silent.

Self-communing whistling that communicates something of unintended significance to the hearer is the subject of Edward Thomas's
poem, "The Penny Whistle."

The new moon hangs like an ivory bugle
In the naked frosty blue;
And the ghylls of the forest, already blackened
By winter, are blackened anew.

The brooks that cut up and increase the forest,
As if they had never known
The sun, are roaring with black hollow voices
Betwixt rage and a moan.

But still the caravan-hut by the hollies
Like a kingfisher gleams between:
Round the mossed old hearths of the charcoal-burners
First primroses ask to be seen.

The charcoal-burners are black, but their linen
Blows white on the line;
And white the letter the girl is reading
Under that crescent fine;

And her brother who hides apart in a thicket,
Slowly and surely playing
On a whistle an olden nursery melody,
Says far more than I am saying.

A seemingly simple lyric, but actually a deeply mysterious and
disturbing one. "The Penny Whistle" is written in traditional ballad
measure (alternative four and three-stress lines rhyming abcb) but

Thomas takes liberties with this, shifting easily between iambic and anapaestic and, once, shortening or eliding a three-stress line to only two stresses ("Blows white on the line"); he also allows the poem's final line to take four rather than three stresses. In short, the form bends under the pressure of Thomas's inner voice, that ruminative utterance so common to his poetry. But why? What is going on? Above all, *why* does the "olden nursery melody" played on a penny whistle say far more than Thomas himself is saying?

The answer has surely to be that the boy's tune tells of what is about to be lost, or so Thomas fears.

For "The Penny Whistle," like so much of Thomas's poetry, is about the deep significance of war. According to Edna Longley, the poem was written early in January, 1915. In July of that year, Thomas would enlist, but that at some level the call to commit himself was already troubling his mind is evident from the opening lines. Longley quotes Thomas quoting Richard Jefferies in the book he wrote about the naturalist writer: "the curved moon hung on the sky as the hunter's horn on the wall." But there is a crucial difference. The "hunter's horn" with which Jefferies compares the moon becomes Thomas's "ivory bugle." In addition, Jefferies' "wall" is replaced by "naked frosty blue." The effect is to suggest not merely an uncertain time of day — late afternoon, presumably though we can't be sure — but some heraldic device, a banner perhaps. But a bugle summons to arms. Besides, although an ivory bugle may suggest something splendid, chivalric — and in 1914 thousands of young men went to war dreaming they would "break a lance in Life's tournament" as the then Prime Minister's son, Herbert Asquith wrote in his poem "The Volunteer"— "naked frosty blue" is far less reassuring. There may be a cold awakening from chivalric dreams. Yet the bugle hangs there, almost as a symbol of some other-worldly insistence, like the cross Constantine saw hanging in the sky. As for the blackened "ghylls of the forest," they hint at an impenetrable darkness, but as though to ward off the words' apocalyptic threat, Thomas, who had, so Longley notes, originally written

105

"gullies," substitutes "ghylls", which, she adds, was usually written as "gills" until "Wordsworth romanticised its spelling."

"Ghylls" is, then, an attempt to sustain the note of romance associated with the ivory bugle, but is itself overset by the voices of brooks pouring through the forest, with their "black hollow voices/Betwixt rage and a moan." For Longley, these voices "blend the natural with the psychological"; they define, she says, "manic-depressive poles." Anyone writing about Thomas will be reluctant to disagree with Longley, whose work has done so much to advance his cause, but it is possible to feel that she rather misses the point here. Admittedly, Thomas suffered from manic-depressive mood swings, but the "roaring" voices he hears in the black forest, while they may bear on his psychological state, also testify to his consciousness of impending voices of war.

> Again the guns disturbed the hour,
> Roaring their readiness to avenge,
> As far inland as Stourton tower,
> And Camelot, and starlit Stonehenge.

This is the last stanza of Thomas Hardy's "Channel Firing," which he dates at the end of the poem as having been written "April 1914." Moreover, the poem appeared in *Satires of Circumstance*, which was published in November of that year. I think it inconceivable that Thomas, a great admirer of Hardy's work, wouldn't have read that poem, especially as in a piece on "War Poetry," which appeared in the journal *Poetry and Drama* in December, 1914, but which will have been written a little earlier, Thomas expressed the hope that Hardy, whose "impersonal song seems to me the best of the time ... may write even better yet." (*Selected Prose of Edward Thomas*, ed. Edna Longley, Carcanet, 1981, p.135.)

It is the "roaring voices," of rage and moan, of fury and suffering, which surely explain the force of "But still the caravan-hut by the hollies/Like a kingfisher gleams between". Longley comments on the fact that "charcoal-burners constructed makeshift cabins in woodland clearings so that they could watch their fires." And she adds that "By 1900, metal kilns had made traditional charcoal-burning a vanishing way of life. 'Mossed old hearths' implies the antiquity of the practice." As antique as Camelot, perhaps, or starlit Stonehenge. The survival of the charcoal-burners is against the odds. But as primroses "ask to be seen," as the kingfisher "gleams" — gone in a flash but perhaps to return — so continuity *may* be possible. Black against white: death or a dying way of life against what may be new growth. "Blows white on the line". There is a skip here, a sudden thrill of energy, emphasised by the assonance. This is nursery rhyme doing its dancing business. And yet the letter the girl reads could well be a letter from a dead lover. And the brother "who hides apart in a thicket" may want to evade the possibility of being recruited. (Conscription only came in at the beginning of 1916, but from August 1914 onwards the pressure on all young men to do the honourable thing and fight was immense.)

None of this can be known, all of it can be inferred. The melody the youth plays on his whistle carries intimations of a way of life under threat from all that is signified by the emblem of that ivory bugle. This is what Henry James meant when, in his essay of 1915, "Within The Rim," he wrote of the imminent threat to the "record of the long safe centuries," though unwisely he put that into words, evoking a merely conventional image of rural England, with its "great trees … gathers in the little bluey-white curtains of the cottage windows … curl of the tinted smoke from the old chimneys." Thomas makes no such mistake. Though his poem is heavy with a sense of foreboding, he allows the whistled melody to say "far more than I am saying," and the dragging rhythm of that last line, together with the extra stress, suggests a weight of significance that Thomas locates in "olden nursery melody" far beyond anything words can express.

VII

Back for a moment to the war in Troy. The question of how Odysseus managed to whistle to Diomedes without arousing the suspicions of the Trojans can't be resolved, but it does allow us to remark that whereas daylight whistling seems habitually reassuring, cheerful, night-time whistling often signals danger. And it does so in at least two senses. The whistler sends a message to alert a companion. But any non-companion who hears the whistling is likely to sense danger lurking in the nearby dark. *Pace* Isherwood, night whistling that starts up out of silence seems fraught with menace. Footsteps echoing in an empty street, a solitary whistler, these are among the hoariest cliches of *film noir*, of radio plays that used to be known as "spine-chillers," and subsequently of television crime series.

Night-time whistling certainly did nothing for Parson Woodforde's peace of mind. "... Andrews the Smuggler brought me this night about 11 o'clock a bagg of Hyson Tea 6Pd weight. He frighted us a little by whistling under the Parlour Window just as we were going to bed. I gave him some Geneva and paid him for the tea at 10/6 per Pd." This Diary entry, dated March 29th, 1777, is typical. Woodforde is repeatedly in a lather about receiving contraband goods, though brandy features more often than tea. Andrews knew his man. "Frighted" though he might be, Woodforde always paid up, and his habitual warm-hearted instinct for hospitality usually led to the offer of a glass of gin (Geneva) for whoever brought him his pipe-tobacco and comestibles. Nevertheless, he was liable to be in a panic while the transactions were taking place. If a smuggler comes can an Excise Man be far behind?

How did Andrews whistle? What sound did he make? "Whistle in your fist." This phrase, which seems to have originated in the 19th century, had wide currency among thieves or was applied to what must have been the distinctive sound they made. Try it. The partly-closed fist acts as an echo-chamber and it isn't difficult to make a whistling sound close to that of an owl's cry, especially the long, wavering call of the tawny or wood-owl. It may well have been this sound, or something like it, which Odysseus used in order to warn Diomedes that it was time for the two of them to be heading back to the Greek ships. The cry of the owl of Minerva, still heard all over Greece, is sharper and little higher than that of any owl cry likely to be heard in Northern Europe, and easy to imitate, even without closed fist. An owl cry can also be used as the signal for attack by night forces, as anyone who has seen war films will know. Blacked-up faces among trees, a glimpse of men crawling on all fours up a hillside, the shaken-out note of an owl, and next moment the spurt of gunfire, the enemy taken by surprise.

An ability to imitate the one bird whose cry belongs to the night is also bound to be extremely useful among thieves. (The night-jar's "purring sound like a sewing-machine working, sometimes continuing without pause for a minute or two" is strictly for the birds.) "The time has been my senses would have cool'd/To hear the night-shriek," the beleagured Macbeth says, and more than one editor has considered the possibility that the shriek comes from animal or bird rather than human and is not necessarily the cry of a victim but of the marauder. But no thief would want to forewarn their intended victim. For this reason, therefore, thieves operating in Burlington Arcade would *not* want to imitate the cry of an owl. They'd need a pattern of daytime whistling in order to communicate with each other. Hence, the implied forbidding of *any* form of whistling there.

VIII

Dickens, that great city walker, knew London at all hours. *Sketches by Boz* includes two essays, "The Streets — Morning" and "The Streets — Night," which teem with the sights and sounds of city life. Apart, that is, from whistling. Street cries, yes, songs, yes, monologue, conversation, argument, yes, yes, and yes again. But for some reason Dickens never mentions whistling. Nor does he have much to say about it where you might most expect to find it, in *Oliver Twist.*

Chapter 21, "The Expedition," which is about how the hapless Oliver accompanies Sikes on his journey up-river to a planned robbery at Shepperton, begins with a description of market-morning at Smithfield.

All the pens in the vast area, and as many temporary pens as could be crowded into the vacant space, were lined with sheep; tied up to posts by the gutter were long lines of beasts and oxen, three or four deep, butchers, drovers, hawkers, boys, thieves, idlers, and vagabonds of every low grade, were mingled together in a mass; the whistling of drovers, the barking of dogs, the bellowing and plunging of oxen, the bleating of sheep, the grunting and squeaking of pigs, the cries of hawkers .... rendered it a stunning and bewildering scene, which quite confounded the senses.

This could easily be a scene from the *Sketches,* which had not long been published and which had brought Dickens a good deal of financial success as well as the confidence to know that his writing — both what he wrote and the way he wrote it — deservedly attracted a wide readership. Perhaps for this reason, there is some-thing almost routine about the description of Smithfield, which for all its imitative verbal higgledy-piggledeness and sustained gerundive clauses, breaks down into unremarkable detail. Still, "The whistling of drovers." At least Oliver is granted the chance to hear that.

The Parish Boy's introduction to "boys, thieves, idlers and vagabonds of every low grade" — far more Dickens's perception that, than Oliver's — occurs, however, much earlier in the novel, when by chance he encounters the Artful Dodger one morning as he makes his escape from the workhouse and strikes out on the road to freedom.

"Going to London?" said the strange boy ....

110

"Yes."

"Got any lodgings?"

"No."

"Money?"

"No."

The strange boy whistled; and put his arms into his pockets, as far as the big coat sleeves would let them. (Chapter 8.)

A whistle of surprise? Disbelief? Of satisfaction? (Here's an innocent I can use.) All three, perhaps.

Late that night, the two finally arrive at the thieves' den, and the Dodger, to make his presence known to the inmates of the house, whistles to gain their attention.

Whistling no doubt cuts through the throng of sounds that pester the night air, "the general blight of the place," including "a good many children, who, even at that time of night, were crawling in and out of doors, or screaming from the inside." Given such a hubbub, it's unlikely the Dodger would have bothered to have whistled in his fist. Still, his whistling is at least a rudimentary form of communication from someone who, the novel makes clear, is as articulate as they come.

Fagin, too, whistles. The following morning, when Oliver wakes "from a sound, long sleep," he sees "The Jew, with his half-closed eyes; heard his low whistling; and recognised the sound of the spoon grating against the saucepan's sides ..." Fagin is furious when he eventually realises that Oliver has been for some time watching him as he studies the stolen goods — "trinkets" — which his boys have brought in. He operates by secrecy, by being close as an oyster. Hence, his low whistling. It is not intended to communicate with anyone or, in this instance, to waken Oliver. Fagin whistles in self-communing isolation, relishing his solitude, his cunning. The sound he makes is as far as he is prepared to go in revealing himself. He certainly doesn't want anyone else to share in his pleasure.

Jean Genet's *Thief's Journal* provides an insight into an altogether more mysterious form of whistling as both self-communing and communication. Genet did not operate as part of a gang of thieves. On the contrary, he held apart from others. And in his prison cell, where he was alone, he writes, he found a strange form of peace.

Prison offered to me the first consolation, the first peace ... Much solitude had forced me to become my own companion. Envisaging the external world, its indefiniteness, its confusion, which is even more perfect at night, I set it up as a divinity ... through painful and exhausting ordeals, to the verge of despair ... the sole object of all this labour ... within me I established this divinity — origin and disposition of myself. I swallowed it. I dedicated to it songs of my own invention. At night I would whistle. The melody was a religious one. It was slow. Its rhythm was somewhat heavy. I thought that I was entering into a communication with God ... God being the only hope and fervour contained in my song. Along the streets, with my hands in my pockets, my head held high looking at houses or trees, I would whistle my clumsy hymns — not joyous, but not sad, either. Sober. I discovered that hope is merely the expression that one gives it. Likewise protection. Never would I have whistled to a light rhythm. I recognised the religious themes: they create Venus, Mercury, or the Virgin.

Genet's whistling appeals to, seeks to communicate with, not merely the supreme protectress of Christianity but the pagan goddess of love and the god of "thieves, pickpockets, and all dishonest persons," in the words of Lemprière's *Classical Dictionary*. Presumably it was this triune God with whom the whistling Genet hoped to make his peace.

There is wit in that "heavy rhythm" — Mercury is a heavy metallic-chemical element. And Venus, though customarily associated with heterosexuality is, as pagan goddess, at least figurally welcoming of gay sexuality. A gay man as well as thief, Genet's whistling is avowedly not conducted "in the fist." It is not in any way secretive. On the contrary, "head held high," he whistles in a manner that combines "hope and fervour." For such a person — perhaps for anyone — the cruellest deprivation is to be denied the chance of utterance.

Not to be allowed to whistle would have driven Wittgenstein mad. In his biography of the philosopher, Ray Monk notes that on one occasion at least Wittgenstein whistled a piece of music rather than giving a lecture, so frustrated was he at not being able to communicate his ideas. And the Mozart scholar, Katherine Thomson, remembered that when in the late 1930s Wittgenstein visited the house in Birmingham where she and her husband, the great classicist and Marxist, George Thomson, lived, their guest would ask her to play Mozart piano sonatas, stop her at a certain point, rush downstairs and out into the street, where they would hear him walking up and down, whistling the passage until he was, as he hoped, note perfect, at which point he would dash back indoors and make her play the passage again, whistling his accompaniment as she did so. Then he would tell her to continue. It may be going too far to say that Wittgenstein's sanity was saved by whistling — it must have tested the sanity of those who had to bear with him — but it does seem that whistling helped him face the world and even in his own strange way communicate with it. According to Monk, Wittgenstein, invited by the Vienna Circle to talk about his Tractatus, whistled a piece of Schubert. For him as for Edward Thomas, whistling said much more than he could say.

No such luck for Genet, who reports that at the age of 15, following a charge of vagrancy, he spent three months in Petite-Roquette prison, a place which in 1836 had been re-modelled along the lines of the panopticon, the "model" prison designed by Bentham and an example of which Dickens had seen in Boston during his American tour of 1842. Such penitentiaries maintained a rule of silence in an attempt to force prisoners into introspection and thus to meditate on God. In Petite-Roquette "the rule of perpetual silence admitted no exceptions. It was forbidden to talk, to sob aloud, to cough too noisily. From one day to the next it was necessary that the most absolute silence reign over the house."

Prisoners whistle to keep their spirits up. But their whistling is also a way of communicating, every bit as useful as tapping out code on pipes or rapping against cell walls. Forbid one and you get the other. Most movingly, Alison Hoffman records that Jews in the various Nazi concentration camps whistled to fight off despair and also to communicate with each other when talk and singing were forbidden. They whistled Yiddish songs and Hoffman tells us that she managed to whistle a snatch of Beethoven's Pastoral Symphony to her husband as the two were separated at Auschwitz. The whistling re-commenced immediately after the war in hospitals and reunion centres. Such whistling not only affirmed survival, it established contact and communication with other survivors.

CODA

In some modern versions of the Bible, including the NIV and the NASB, God is said to whistle to his people. This is understandable. He is the Great Shepherd. And so in *Isaiah*, Chapter 7, Verse 18, according to NIV, God whistles "for flies from the distant streams of Egypt and for bees from the land of Assyria." Flies and bees are said to be symbols of God's judgement. Josiah was killed and afterwards Judah had only weak kings. The Egyptians captured Josiah's son and the next king, Jehoiakim, was captured by Nebuchadnezzer and taken to Babylon. But in *Zecharaiah* Chapter 10, Verse 8, God announces that he will "whistle for them [his people] to gather together. For I have redeemed them. And they will be as numerous as they were before." There are other references to God's whistling scattered thinly throughout the Old Testament, at least in the versions identified above. For example *Judges* Chapter 5, Verse 16 and *Isaiah* Chapter 5 Verse 26.

But in the King James Bible, which is what was read in England after 1611, God doesn't whistle. Instead, he either "pipes," as he does in *Judges* Chapter 5, Verse 16, — "Why satest thou among the sheepfolds/To hear the pipings for the flocks," or he "hisses," as in *Isaiah* 5, 26 — "and he will lift up an ensign to the nations from afar, and will hiss for them from the end of the earth", and again at 7, 18, "the lord shall hiss for the fly that is in the uttermost part of the rivers of Egypt ..."

Hissing is what God usually does. Whether the ancient Greek for the verb to hiss was the same as the verb to whistle is therefore irrelevant. Nor need we speculate as to whether God's hissing suggests that the Almighty's whistling was at fault. In the Bible everyone in England read, God may be the Great Shepherd but he certainly doesn't communicate with his people by whistling to them. And bearing in mind his customary anger, not to say contempt, for their backsliding, to say that he hissed seems far more plausible.

Whistling as Protest
and Resistance

I

In his *Jazz Anecdotes,* Bill Crow reports on a gig the blind multi-instrumentalist, Ronald Kirk, played at Ronnie Scott's Club. This was in the days when the Club still hadn't bothered to obtain a proper drinks licence and as a result was on more than one occasion raided by the police.

> Roland was doing that pennywhistle thing. He distributed about a hundred pennywhistles to the audience, and everyone was blowing like mad. It was like a madhouse. About twenty plain-clothes men and women came in. And no one took a bit of notice. Just went on blowing, like an aviary. Roland couldn't see what was happening, of course, just thundered on. All this law trying to get names and addresses. Policeman say to me, "Go up and tell him to stop." I said, "*You* go up and tell him to stop."
> (OUP, New York, p. 282.)

It's possible that Crow doesn't fully understand the incident he vividly reports. Yes, the audience at first whistled in a kind of joyous mayhem, but once they realised that the club had been raided by the police — so often regarded as the natural enemy of jazz, of anything that takes a walk on the wild side — the whistling became shrilly concentrated in protest at the actions of the plain-

116

clothes officers. The mass whistling was now an uninhibited protest against the Law.

The whistlers in Ronnie Scott's Club weren't showing their disapproval of Roland Kirk. Far from it. They were on his side, as they were on the side of the Club's host. But this is far from typical of the whistling that occasionally rises in theatre or club land. More often in such places, whistling is a sign of dissatisfaction with or disapproval of the performer(s). There are other such signs. Booing, catcalls, shouting rude or derisive comments, the slow handclap, the sound of seats being tipped up as the audience takes its leave. But professional entertainers go in special dread of the disapproving whistle. According to Mervyn Gould, for some years during the 1960s front-of-house manager at Sunderland Empire, whistling was the professional entertainer's death. "You see, petal, if someone shouts at you, you can always shout back. Life on the boards teaches you how to deal with hecklers. I've even known a comedian who was going down badly turn on those booing him, but then he was top of the bill and the chances are that those who boo.e.d. were planted in the audience. Boo a mother-in-law joke and you can become the butt of stage humour. 'I see we've got a representative from the League Against Cruel Sports in the audience. If you think what I say is cruel you should hear my mother-in-law's husband. Oh, no, too late. He died some years ago. He said it was the only way he'd be sure to get some peace.' Well, we didn't say it was funny. But there's no comeback against whistling. Get yourself off stage as fast as you can, that's what any old pro will tell you. And never offer to play Glasgow on a wet Monday night. The best whistlers in the world can be found in the front row of the stalls at Glasgow Empire."

Such whistling can often be unfair. In 1956 Louis Armstrong's All-Stars played their first concerts in the UK after the Musicians Union lifted its twenty-year old ban against foreign bands being employed here. (Individual musicians were welcome but they had to be accompanied by the home-grown product.) The organisers, who had little or no understanding of the reverence in which

Armstrong was held by jazz followers, arranged a concert bill at the Empress Hall which began with half-an-hour from a large, fairly stodgy "swing" outfit, The Vic Lewis Orchestra. Next up, Peg-Leg Bates, a good tap-dancer, but not someone the packed audience had come to see. Still less was it prepared for the woman singer, Ella Logan, who followed Peg-Leg. Where was Louis Armstrong? Even before she opened her mouth the whistling began. Poor woman, it wasn't her fault. She struggled on for some ten minutes before giving up. By then the whistling had become so overpowering it's doubtful whether she could hear the sound of her own voice.

After this opening-night fiasco, the organisers replaced the Vic Lewis orchestra by Humphrey Lyttleton's band, whose devotion to the music Armstrong pioneered was bound to be more to the audience's taste, and though they kept Peg-Leg Bates on the bill, the singer disappeared. A pity, perhaps, given that in George Melly's apt summing up, the woman vocalist with the All-Stars, Velma Middleton, "made up in bulk what she lacked in swing." She was frankly dire. She *should* have been whistled at.

Protest whistling is also a feature of what is sometimes called "legitimate" theatre. When the Duke of York reports to his wife on the tepid reception the crowd gave to Richard II compared with the effect Bolingbroke made, he famously notes that "As in a theatre the eyes of men,/After a well graced actor leaves the stage,/Are idly bent on him that enters next,/Thinking his prattle tedious," so is it with Richard. As so often, Shakespeare is here delighting in the possibilities the play gives him. The speaker is himself an actor, and in a sense he's taking the audience on, telling them that they shouldn't treat him as badly as the bystanders he's mentioned — the groundlings — have treated Richard. What Shakespeare's audience would have been well aware of, would indeed have relished, is precisely the chance to protest against tedious prattle. Such protest can include whistling, as seems must be the case in *Coriolanus,* where the crowd's reaction to the protagonist's contempt for them — "You common cry of curs" — is to make a medley of sounds, of whoops, hoots and skirls, among which whistling is surely present. In other words, Shakespeare brings on stage the sounds Coriolanus's Roman enemies indulge in and by such means confronting his audience with its own questionable manners.

Not that this can be expected to silence whistling, any more than whistlers can be silenced in the opera house. There seems good reason to suppose that opera audiences are the rowdiest, most unmannerly of all In *A Room With a View*, E.M. Forster treats this unmannerliness as social comedy, even an endorsement of southern warmth as opposed to the frozen rectitude of northern Europeans; and this is also the view of D.H. Lawrence in his account of a visit to the opera in *Twilight in Italy*. But the storms of protest that often greet productions thought to defame a particular opera can go so far as to bring performances to a standstill. And among the boos, catcalls, and cries of horror, whistling is certain to make itself heard.

II

It's a moot point whether protest whistling in the theatre is brought in from elsewhere or precedes such whistling. But an enclosed space undoubtedly makes whistling more resonant and therefore more effective. It may be for this reason that while whistling is common at Association and Rugby football matches, as it is at boxing and wresting halls, you hardly ever hear it at cricket matches. This can hardly be because such unmannerly behaviour is agreed to be "not cricket." Cricketing crowds boo what they see as unsporting behaviour. (No Nottinghamshire supporter will ever forgive Geoffrey Boycott for the inexcusably selfish running-out of Derek Randall at Randall's home ground of Trent Bridge during the 1978 Test match, Randall's first appearance there as an England player.) Spectators make plain their displeasure at tedious passages of play by means of the slow handclap; and derisive, shouted comment at a badly-dropped catch or piece of maladroit fielding is common enough. "Put your hands together, vicar, and pray," was the suggestion of an Australian supporter in Sydney while the Revd. David Shepherd, not an especially good fielder, waited under a ball that came spiralling out of the blue. (He dropped it.) But though someone may occasionally blow a mechanical whistle, crowd whistling at cricket is virtually unknown. This can only be because it simply isn't effective in the wide open spaces of a cricket ground. The sound doesn't carry.

Nevertheless, whistling is a device understandably used by anti-hunt campaigners. Its intention is to confuse the dogs and, more generally, to add to the hubbub of sounds that bear some comparison with the noises produced as part of a skimmington ride. For skimmington rides, those ludicrous, sometimes socially vicious processions through a village in which men and women to be humiliated — a nagging or unfaithful wife, an adulterous husband, seated arsy-versy on a donkey (one features in *The Mayor of Casterbridge*) — were accompanied by what social historians call Rough Music. The poet Arnold Rattenbury itemised this as "a mixture of pot-banging, horn-blowing, hooting, fence-rattling, shouting, roaring, banging the hell out of whatever is in reach", and of course it including whistling, both human and mechanical.

Rough Music, Rattenbury says, who is writing about rural custom in the 18th century, accompanies just about every rural occasion: "bounds-beating, all the tests and trials called Ridings, Bee Customs (chiefly bringing the bees to swarm), apprentice rituals, procession of prisoners to jail and intruders beyond the bounds ...". (See "Methodism and Tatterdermalions, in *Popular Culture and Class Conflict, 1590-1914*, ed S. and E. Yeo, 1981.)

But at this point the connection between whistling, protest, and politics, requires some comment.

III

One of the best plays staged at the Edinburgh Fringe in 1977 was *Whistling at Milestones*. Written by Alex Glasgow, though never, it seems, published, the play was performed by Pirate Jenny Theatre Company, one of the many groups that regularly toured towns and villages through the kingdom during the 1970s and 80s, playing venues both large and small, sometimes very small indeed; all these groups were, however loosely, identified with what used to be called Agit-Prop Theatre. *Whistling at Milestones* is about the Jarrow March of 1936 — "The Jarrow Crusade" as it became widely known — when 200 unemployed workers walked from their home in the North East to London in order to present a petition to Parliament demanding that the government of the day should do something for a town where well over fifty percent of the work force had no paid labour. Initially the Government announced that it would refuse to receive the petition but in the end accepted it on condition that the petition wasn't handed in by the men themselves. Such magnanimity. The marchers were tricked into going on a river boat trip while their document was handed over (not officially presented) to Baldwin's Government of National Unity, which, given that the March was made deliberately non-political, was the least they could do. Backers included the local MP Ellen Wilkinson ("Red Ellen," named as much for the colour of her hair as for her fiery left-wing politics), and a number of Conservative Party officials agreed to help organize the march.

Some of this inevitably feeds into Glasgow's play. But its focus is on the men — seven of them — who are made the spokespersons not merely for the marchers but for Jarrow and, more generally, the Rights of Labour. Glasgow also brings vividly to life the contrasting responses of the various people in villages and towns on whom the marchers are billeted as they make their increasingly foot-weary trek south: responses that encompass at one extreme frosty disapproval, even disdain, and, at the other, generous welcome. To put the matter this way is to risk making the play sound like mere propaganda. In fact, its success depends entirely on Glasgow's ability to reveal the men as individuals brought together by the crusade itself. It's difficult to think that someone associated with the film, *The Full Monty*, about unemployed men from Sheffield's collapsed steel industry in the 1980s, wasn't aware of Glasgow's play, although the film's feel-good factor prevents it from having the political edge and bite of *Whistling at Milestones*.

What symbolises, or, more accurately perhaps, *expresses* the Jarrow men's united beliefs and commitment, is the music they play as they march. The songs they sing, often to the accompaniment of a mouth-organ, the tunes they whistle. Whistling at milestones keeps their spirits high. We've got this far and we're still on track. We'll get there. The whistling is both protest at the government's indifference to the plight of the town the men have left behind them and an assertion of their resilience, their refusal to be broken by those like the unspeakable Lord Runciman, President of the Board of Trade, who proclaimed that Jarrow should be left to its own devices.

IV

The whistling of the Jarrow marchers may have been in part a form of protest against unemployment but it was orderly and no doubt harmonious. The same is almost certain to have been true of all those who were on the various marches of the NUWM (National Unemployed Workers' Movement) and other, similar, marches organised by and for working men which are a feature of the period 1920-40. Many of these marches were led by what were euphemistically called "Jazz Bands." In his warmly affectionate memoir of a working-class childhood in South Wales, *Up The Lamb*, the late John Ackerman recalls that at the time of the 1926 General Strike, "jazz bands were popular in the mining valleys." Judging from newspaper photographs of some of the marches, though, the instrumentation of these essentially marching bands

122

was rudimentary, do-it-yourself. Snare drums, kazoos, paper-and-comb, even rolled-up newspapers. And, of course, penny whistles or, for some marchers, their own efforts at mouth-whistling.

"Jazz" in this context meant less a specific kind of music than an attitude, and it's not surprising that during the miners' strike of 1984-85 "Jazz Bands" returned as features of protest marches. Nothing had changed: the same instrumentation, the same readiness, if not ability, to use snare drums, kazoos, tin trumpets and whistles in order to generate marching tunes and a beat you could swing along to. These "jazz bands" were plainly descendents of the Rough Music Arnold Rattenbury writes about, though sufficiently well ordered to help rather than hinder the marchers.[1]

V

But what is orderly to some can seem threatening to others. It's all, you might say, in the ear of the listener. Hence, the following:

> More and more, because of our blind faith in machinery, because of our want of light to enable us to look beyond machinery to the end for which machinery is valuable, this and that man, and this and that body of men, all over the country, are beginning to put in practice an Englishman's right to do what he likes; his right to march where he likes, meet where he likes, enter where he likes, hoot as he likes, threaten as he likes, smash as he likes.

These words come from the section called "Doing as One Likes" in Matthew Arnold's *Culture and Anarchy*, first published in book form in 1869. Over the Christmas period, 2012-13, BBC4 ran a series of programmes about "Culture," presented by the ubiquitous Melvyn Bragg, during which Arnold was used as a touchstone by more or less all of the contributors, and yet nobody, not a soul, mentioned that Arnold was spurred into writing the book, which started life as lectures, because of the Hyde Park Riots, the first of which occurred in July, 1866, and the following a year later. The Reform League, which was campaigning for universal male suffrage, was banned from meeting in the Park and indeed the Park was declared out of bounds for all public meetings. In his account of these events, to be found in *The English Rebel: One Thousand Years of Troublemaking from the Normans to the Nineties,* David Horspool says that the League's response to this ukase was to organise a march to the Park where "a section of the crowd turned violent, breaking down the railings and fighting with the police. A second meeting the following the following year defied a government ban, gathering up 200,000 people peacefully to hear speeches on reform."

"Fighting with the police" is studiously neutral, but anyone who recalls the actual course of events at Orgreave during the 1984/5 miners'strike will have no difficulty in believing that the fighting was unlikely to have been begun by the marchers. The men who wanted to hold a meeting in Hyde Park could hardly be said to have had a blind faith in machinery. Among them would have been plenty opposed to the fact that machinery was, as they knew all too well, threatening, even supplanting their chances of employment. It's a fair bet that some, perhaps many, would have been familiar with the inside of Mechanics' Institutes, where they could hear "improving" lectures, good music, and enlightened discussions on those cultural matters Arnold champions. Many of them had learnt foreign languages, read "the classics," saw performances of Shakespeare's plays, attended concerts and, where they could, visited art galleries and museums. They were far from being the unwashed ignoramuses Arnold depicts as needing to be rescued from their own darkness by a programme of sweetness and light, though some of the dimmer contributors to Bragg's programmes clearly took for granted working-class or "popular" culture as still mired in the "anarchy" of Arnold's formulation. What caused so many men in 1866 and again in 1867 to march to Hyde Park and there, perhaps, to riot, was not their desire for anarchy, still less their indifference to culture; what motivated them was a determination that the Park shouldn't be enclosed by railings, that it should continue to be open to everyone as it had been at the time of the Great Exhibition, and that it should be available to those who wanted to use it for public meetings.

As the men marched, so, according to Arnold, they "hooted." The word has a history. "To shout in contempt," Johnson says, and he cites Sidney. "A number of country folks happened to pass by, who hollowed and hooted after me as at the arrantest coward." The O.E.D., dating the word back to the late middle ages, defines its meaning as "a loud, inarticulate exclamation, a shout, *spec.* of derision or disapproval." As already noted, the crowd that drives Coriolanus out of Rome "hoot" and "whoop." "Hoot" is therefore closely linked to sounds not merely of protest but protest made by those who lack power: "country folks", the Roman Crowd. Such noise is a part of popular protest. The men who marched in protest to Hyde Park were making noises that scared Arnold, and there seems no reason to doubt that whistling would have featured among the sounds they made (an owl's hoot is also an owl's whistle), just as whistling is among the sounds made by those who protest against hunting wild animals. Whistling was an accomplishment common to working men. Besides, you can whistle in derision quite as effectively as you can hoot.

You also take heart from whistling with others. The lone protest whistler is unlikely to be effective, simply because he/she isn't part of an audible crowd, isn't therefore making a popular protest. Hence, perhaps the clerk in John Davidson's famous poem of the 1890s, "Thirty Bob A Week."

I step into my heart and there I meet
A god-almighty devil singing small,
Who would like to shout and whistle in the street,
And squelch the passer flat against the wall;

125

If the whole world was a cake he had the power to take,
He would take it, ask for more, and eat them all.

But being on his own he lacks the power and so sings small and
daren't whistle, for what, without others to join him, would be the
point? Davidson, who knew all about the struggles for survival, in
his case as a jobbing writer, was by temperament incapable of
surrendering the conviction that the strong deserve to triumph, the
weak to fail.

VII

In 1699 the Benedictine Monastery of St. Waldrine in France rang
to the shrill, unified whistling of monks as they protested at the
teachings of St. Thomas Aquinas, which they were daily fed. The
monks, who had been reading Descartes, were no longer prepared
to accept Aquinas's account of the universe which the Abbot
wished to enforce. They were fed up. And so they began to whistle.
This example of resistance to authority, whether religious or
secular, is one that can be replicated at just about any point in
history. For instance, during the period when Mussolini's fascist
party governed Italy, the National hymn of Sardinia (Hymnu
Soudu) was whistled on the streets as a form of protest against the
dictator's refusal to allow any other language than Italian to be
spoken throughout the Italian mainland and islands. You might not
be allowed to sing the Sardinian words but you could at least imply
them in what you whistled.

Another instance. In his poem "Santa Espina," Louis Aragon
writes;

I remember a tune which was whistled at night
In a sunless time, an age with no wandering knight
When children wept for the bombs and in catacombs
A noble people dreamt of the tyrants' doom.

In the poem's middle stanzas Aragon imagines the whistled tune as an eloquent symbol of resistance to all kinds of suffering, from that of "a god as he hung upon the gallows", to that of peoples who, for all the repression and injustice they endure, refuse to abandon the spirit of resistance, the vision of freedom, who internalise these and thus keep them alive. The poem ends:

I would like to believe that there is music still
In that country's heart, though hidden underground
The dumb will speak and the paralytics will
March one fine day to the cobla's triumphant sound

Whistling and humming a tune whose words people know even if they may not utter them is a form of resistance as well as a way of taking heart. And in what is really a companion poem, "Richard Coeur-de-Lion," Aragon has the immured king "watch the swallow fly/Who speaks to heaven a language under ban." The swallow's song is a whistle of joyous freedom. The poem ends, "All Frenchmen are Blondel, in each he sings:/Whatever name we called her at the start/Freedom — like a whispering of wings —/Answers the song of Richard Lionheart." Blondel was Richard's companion who in legend wandered through the land where the king was imprisoned, singing a ballad outside each prison in order to reveal his presence. Finally, he came to the prison where Richard lay. It may even be that he whistled like a swallow to let the king know of his presence. Troubadours were said to be privy to the language of the birds.

Another instance. "Chant des Partisans" was a song written and performed by Anna Marly for French Resistance fighters and broadcast from London during the second world war. Marly, who was born into an aristocratic family in St. Petersburg in 1917, and whose birth name was Anna Betoulinky, made her way to Paris some time after her father was shot by the Bolsheviks, married a Dutchman, and in 1940 arrived in London, having escaped from

France in the nick of time. In her autobiography, *Anna Marly: Troubador de Resistance* (1980), she recalls working as a volunteer during the Blitz, "picking up arms, legs, a traumatic experience." She began performing her own songs, in French, English, Russian and Polish for Allied service men, and in particular broadcast from London on the *Honour and Homeland* programme intended for the French Resistance. Two of her compositions, "Song of the Partisans" and "Complaint of the Partisan," ("Complainte" in French means both "ballad" and "lament"), which were written or anyway broadcast in 1943, became especial favourites, so much so, that the RAF dropped leaflets with the lyrics printed on them all over rural France.

Marly didn't merely sing. She whistled the tunes of her songs because whistling was thought to cut through the static Germans used to try to jam the broadcasts. According to one story, five Resistance fighters captured by the Germans and ordered to dig their own graves whistled the tune of one of Marly's songs as they wielded their spades. The story is known because one of the men managed to escape. French Resistance fighters also sang and whistled Marly's songs over the hastily-dug graves of dead comrades.

In the English version, the first and last of the five stanzas of "Complaint" run:

When they poured across the border
I was cautioned to surrender.
This I could not do,
I took my gun and vanished ....

Oh the wind, the wind is blowing
Through the graves the wind is blowing,
Freedom soon will come
It will come from the shadows.

And the first and last of the four stanzas of "Song" are as follows:

Friend, do you hear the crow's dark flight over our plains?
Friend, do you hear the muffled cries of the land being shelled?
Ahoy! Resistants, workers and farmers, the alarm has sounded,
Tonight the enemy shall know the price of blood and tears ....

Here each one of us knows what he wants, what he does when he
     passes by.
Friend, if you fall, a friend comes from the shadows in your place.
Tomorrow, black blood will dry in the sun on the roads.
Sing, companions, in the night freedom listens to us.

The words became so well known among Resistance fighters that it
was enough for Marly to begin to whistle the tune for the words to
come to mind, to hearten and sustain the men and women listening
to her. "In the night freedom listens to us."

Another instance. In 1948 some sixteen hundred boys began to
whistle in a Prague sports stadium in protest at the Communist
takeover of Czechoslovakia, and the tune they whistled then was
taken up and repeatedly used during the years of oppression
following the Prague Spring of 1968. This mass whistling is common
to soldiers the world over who, accustomed to whistle in support of
political or military masters as they march in line to such tunes as
"The White Cockade," "Yankee Doodle Dandy," or "Colonel
Bogey," can also whistle them in opposition to the perceived
enemy, especially if that enemy is taking them into captivity. And
anyone listening to the televised speech Ceausescu made in
December 1989 from the balcony of the Communist Party head-
quarters in the centre of Bucharest — a speech that began with
arrogant certainty and ended in bewildered retreat and his later
execution — will hear, among the gathering cat-calls and jeers,
increasingly derisive whistles that swell the sounds of protest.

A more ambiguous instance. In the United States, the black man
Emmett Till's wolf-whistle brought about his lynching by white
men. But the racist brutality of Till's murder helped lead to the

founding of the Civil Rights movement. His was not a protest whistle, but at least it can be said that it caused a protest movement whose consequences for black people were enormous.

And another, previously mentioned, but deserving of being repeated here. Jews in concentration camps were refused the chance to sing . As a result, they whistled. The whistling was no doubt a form of comfort, of self-communing, as well as of communication, a way of keeping their collective spirits up. But it will also have been a form of protest at the refusal to allow them the right to song. After the war, survivors often whistled tunes that had become familiar to them in the camps, no longer in protest, but in an attempt to re-connect with now lost family and friends.

As to the Cretan shepherds who, like the people of Aas, during WWII whistled to warn resistance groups of the presence of Nazi troops, such whistling was at once message and protest, and sometimes resulted in their being shot. It was also a form of resistance, and as such is glancingly relevant to the argument Jacques Attali advances in *Noise: The Political Economy of Music,* in which he points out that music as resistance can be found in the middle ages across Europe where "independent jongleurs composed satirical songs about current affairs, and kings would forbid them to sing about certain delicate subjects, under threat of imprisonment." Forbidden to sing, you whistled, though that didn't always save you. The Cretan shepherds who did their best to save resistance fighters from the Nazis often whistled Cretan folk tunes as a warning. What could be more innocent? What could be more loaded with meaning?

Note

[1] For more of "jazz bands" as they took part in protest marches, often leading them, see "Jazz on the March", by John Lucas, in *The Penniless Press,* Issue 21, Spring, 2005. It should be said that in the UK real jazz bands, especially those associated with Ken Colyer and all who played his kind of New Orleans music, led a number of CND marches from the late 1950s on, and were often part of TUC parades.

Nowadays samba bands often replace the jazz bands, their leaders, in grand and perhaps parodic imitation of drum majors, using mechanical whistles to give commands to the musicians. Such whistles are also used, to deafening effect, by demonstrators as well as those participating in marches and processions at Caribbean Carnivals.

Whistling as Entertainment

I

As with whistling at and for work, so whistling to entertain others goes back a long way. But we need to distinguish between entertainment provided for free, on the one hand, and, on the other, whistling as a profession. Professional whistling is performed before a paying audience or recorded and offered for sale. Whistling acts became a common staple of music hall during the latter half of the 19th century and first half of the 20th. And once the record industry got going, whistling was taken into the recording studio. Whistling on street corners and for cinema and theatre queues was also a common feature of town and city life; and there were whistling buskers.

This has to be put in the past tense because it's far from certain that such whistling survives in all but stray outposts. The poet Simon Curtis recalls a moment in the early years of the present century when he came across a busking violinist in a Stockport underpass playing and whistling the old folk tune "Devil Among the Tailors"; and at about the same time you could sometimes pass a middle-aged Black busker who used his pitch outside Green Park tube station on Piccadilly for whistling as he tap-danced. There are one or two other such survivals, but by and large street whistling as paid entertainment has dwindled to near nothingness.

Yet in the nineteenth century street whistlers were a common feature of town and city. In writing about London Characters, Henry Mayhew notes that "It sometimes happens that a lad or man, before being thrown for a living on the streets, has often sung a song to amuse his companions, or that he has been reckoned 'a good whistler,' so he resolves to start out and see if he cannot turn to pecuniary profits that which until now had only been regarded in the light of an amusement." Mayhew records an interview with one such whistler.

I am a whistler — that is, I whistle with my lips without the aid of anything beside. I have been at it about seven years. I am twenty next birthday .... As I could always whistle very well, I thought I'd try it for a living; so I made a pitch in New Street, Covent Garden, and began by whistling 'Will You Love Me Then as Now.' .... I did very well that day, for I got about 3s. 6d or 4s; so I thought I'd practice it and stick to it. I worked all about town till I got well known. I used to sometimes go into public houses and whistle upon a piece of 'baccy' pipe, blowing into the bowl, and moving my fingers as if I was playing a flute and nobody could tell the difference if they had not seen me. Sometimes I used to be asked to stand outside hotels, taverns, and even club-houses, and give 'em a tune: I often had sixpences, shillings, and even half-crowns thrown to me.

Good enough pickings, but as the whistler adds, "It's very tiring work, and makes you precious hungry, when you keep at it for two or three hours; and I only wish I could get something else to do." Meanwhile, he tells Mayhew, he has polished and broadened his repertoire to include such favourites as "The Mariner's Grave," "Lucy Neal," "The Barley Stack" (much in demand from country folk up in town for the day), and "Ben Bolt," which he said was one of those "liked best in the streets."

Mayhew also reports a whistler who told him that whistling was thirsty work. Wetting your whistle, in other words, was essential to the performer.

A gentleman came up to me once in the street that was a doctor, and asked me whether I drunk much, and whether I drawed my breath or blowed it out. I told him I couldn't get much to drink, and he said I ought to have at least three pints of beer a day, or else I should go into a consumption; and when I said I mostly blowed out when I whistled, he said that was best, because it didn't strain the lungs so much.

Three pints of beer a day. Is that so? Impossible not to imagine the street whistler looking hard at Mayhew as he relayed this significant bit of medical opinion. You couldn't see your way to buying me a pint, could you, guv'nor? Guard against a fit of consumption. Mayhew, being a well-meaning soul, probably paid up.

Anyway, his conscience may have goaded him into putting his hand in his pocket. For he is on record as claiming that street whistling took its toll. He describes one street whistler as having a long, thin face, and cheeks "so hollowed out by whistling, that they appeared almost to have a round piece of flesh scooped out of them." Not only that, his lips "were generally kept half-an-inch apart, so that they gave him a half idiotic look; and when he rounded them for whistling, they reminded me somewhat of a lamb's kidney."

All credit to Mayhew's powers of observation, though it isn't easy to go along with his view that the evidence of declining health — "whistler's lips" or, indeed "whistler's cheeks" — is an occupational hazard. More likely, the poor man was tubercular. Or undernourished. Or not getting his three pints of beer a day.

But there were occasional compensations. One street whistler recalls for Mayhew's benefit that when he was whistling in front of a gentleman's house "down at Hounslow", the gentleman sent his servant to call the whistler in.

I was taken into a fine large room, full of looking glasses, and time pieces, and pictures. The gentleman was there with all his family — about six on 'em — and he told me that if I'd whistle and learn his birds to sing, he'd give me a sovereign. He had three fine brass-wire cages, with a bird in each, slung all of a row from the ceiling. I set to work like a 'brick,' the birds began to sing directly, and I amused 'em all very much. I stopped about an hour and a half, and let 'em have all sorts of tunes, and then he gave me a sovereign and told me to call again when I come that way; but before I left he said the servants was to give me something to eat and drink, so I had dinner in the kitchen with the servants, and a jolly good dinner it was.

The whistler's ability to teach birds to sing is at one with an episode of *Tess of the D'Urbevilles* discussed earlier in this book, and, as Gilbert White's testimony, also touched on in these pages reveals, must have once been common practice. But like street whistling itself teaching cage birds to whistle has more or less vanished, as have the cage birds (thank goodness). Gone, too, are those fiddlers who were hired for village dances, and who supplemented their playing with whistling which was often more melodious and accurate than their work on the violin. One of us was told by his mother of an old man who in the late 1920s played for dances and at parties in the then tiny Huntingdon village of Sawtry, where she visited a girl cousin. "Whatever he was asked to play, he said 'right ho.' But often he'd have to stop playing and whistle the tune. His playing wasn't up to much, but he could whistle like Billy-o."

So could the 19th century professional cricketer, George Ulyett (1851-1898 — he died after catching pneumonia while he watched Yorkshire play Kent at Bramhall Lane, Sheffield.) An all-rounder who opened the batting for both county and country, bowled fast round-arm and was a good field, Ulyett went on numerous MCC tours, including Australia (three times), South Africa, and North America. This last, as the compilers of *Who's Who of Cricketers* sniffily inform us, was not a first-class tour, but Ulyett was one of the first names to be pencilled in. The reason was simple: his whistling kept the changing-room in good spirits. Ulyett would undoubtedly have been chosen to play Test cricket on his cricketing merits alone. At the time of his death he was widely regarded as the greatest Yorkshire batsman, ever. But his whistling prowess was equally unchallenged. Such music is nowadays surplus to requirement. iPods provide all the music a changing room needs.

II

Music hall, too, has virtually died. And it's difficult to imagine that the entertainment managers of the few working-men's clubs that linger on ever think of booking a whistling act. With the honourable exception of Sheila Harrod, of whom more later, Ronnie Ronalde was probably the last of his kind. He was a radio "star" for some years after WWII and regularly featured on "light entertainment" programmes such as Variety Bandbox, often appearing high up on the bill. Sometimes, he topped it. His signature tune, "If I was a Blackbird", much imitated by street whistlers, became a best-selling record. The B Side was "Bells Across the Meadow," a tune of saccharine sweetness to which Ronalde, aided by sweeping strings and even, if memory serves, a tolling bell, did full justice. At the time, that is the 1940s and early 50s, you could hear men in street and pub trying to imitate the Ronalde sound. Others enjoyed parodying it, but then parody can be every bit as much a form of flattery as imitation. And to enable imitation, there was even a Ronnie Ronalde "whistle aid" on sale in toy shops and tobacconists. Shaped rather like a polo mint but made of tin, it was meant to be placed between your teeth while you blew through its hole.

In *Knocking Down Ginger*, his memoir of life in London's East End and beyond, the socialist John Gorman tells a good anecdote about Ronalde. Gorman and Lionel Begleiter (soon to become better known as Lionel Bart), had chummed up while doing their National Service and, once back on Civvy Street, decided to open a printing works in

136

London's East End. By 1956 they were doing well enough to require new premises, which they found in Hackney. Soon after their move, they decided to convert the open space they had taken over into an office and studio, and so, early one Sunday morning, arrived to make the necessary alterations. The place was, Gorman says, "as quiet as a cemetery." But when they left four hours later, "the road was jam packed, nose to tail with private cars. ... Why were they there?" The mystery was solved when the two men went into the nearby pub which, "practically empty all week ... was filled to capacity." it turned out to be "a rendezvous for homosexuals from all over London." (The legalising of homosexuality was still some years in the future.) "There was a compere on stage, known to everyone by his pseudonym of 'Gaye,' with gorgeous wavy hair and a heavily powdered face, wearing a white silk blouse and the tightest trousers I had ever seen, openly camping his way through a routine of *double entendre* patter as he alternated between singing and introducing the next act. Radio stars Carol Levis and Ronnie Ronalde appeared, as did a variety of drag queens." (pp. 179-180). Well, good for Ronalde.

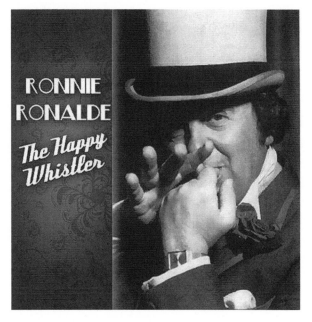

III

Ronalde is almost at the end of the line of whistlers as popular entertainers. Add in Percy Edwards, who for years had regular work on BBC radio as a kind of one-man sound effects studio for all things natural — from dogs to blackbirds — and you have virtually exhausted the names of those who used their skills as whistlers to make money as "artistes."

One other name, though, needs to be added, that of Sheila Harrod. Sheila, a supremely talented whistler who lives in rural Nottinghamshire, first came to the attention of audiences as a young teenager in the 1950s, when, prompted by her father, she stood on a stool in a Working Men's Club in Leicester and wowed the members with some spectacular fingers-in-mouth whistling. The technique involves thrusting the first three fingers of her right hand inside the mouth, cupping the left over the fingers to act as a "hood" or tympan, and letting rip.

Sheila was born with an unusually high roof to her mouth, which prompted the midwife who attended her birth to prophesy that in due course she might well develop into a singer with a wide vocal range and "carry." As matters turned out, Sheila's expertise in whistling was considerably enhanced by the sheer volume of sound the high roof, like a mini-cathedral vault, made possible. But though nature provided the volume, it was hours of arduous practice that gave Sheila her extraordinary technique, and although she is adamant that she can't manage the triple-tonguing of many brass players, some of them would at least envy her trills and wide vibrato. These carefully-honed skills, combined with a well-chosen repertoire and presentational flair, led to her being voted World Champion Whistler in a competition for men and women held some years ago in Berlin, and she is still readily acknowledged as one of the finest practitioners of her art, having entertained in major cities throughout Europe, from Norway to Switzerland.

138

Sheila Harrod

World Whistling Champion !

Første konsert i Skandinavia !

På Villa Fridheim, onsdag 26. August

Kl. 18.30   *Billett kr. 180,-*

For years Sheila was accompanied by a pianist, but out-of-tune pianos in clubs and on stage have in more recent times forced her to switch to the use of backing tapes. Many of the clubs where she once worked have closed their doors, as have most of the variety theatres where she began her career. But she still has regular employment in Britain and abroad, especially Germany, Cyprus (the army base), and Scandinavian countries, often dressed as Marie Lloyd, especially when she performs "My Old Man (said follow the van)"; and for some time now she has been in demand at funerals, where her renditions of "The Old Rugged Cross", "A Closer Walk With Thee", and, especially, "The Londonderry Air", are regularly requested. "I come cheaper than bagpipes," she says, not altogether seriously.

Are there any other whistlers on the circuit, we asked her. Sheila mentioned a siffleuse called "Dottie Mayne." But this one performer apart, there was, she thought nobody but herself left to carry on the tradition of professional whistling in the UK.

Yet whistling as paid entertainment is to be heard in other European countries as well as in the USA. Whistling groups are especially popular in the mid-southern states, part of country-and-western music, whereas in Norway, Germany, Austria and Switzerland, individual whistlers are more often to be found treading the boards of live theatres or, even, performing in television studios. But overall the heyday of professional whistling is without doubt coterminous with the heyday of music hall and of variety artists, a period lasting from the 1880s through to the advent of cinema. The decline set in once talkies arrived, although in the UK it was to some extent arrested by working-men's clubs and holiday camps, where comedians, singers, jugglers, magicians, contortionists, and whistlers could land regular bookings. It is now virtually at an end.

As an expression of popular culture Music Hall has deservedly received a good deal of study, from, among others, Peter Bailey, the socialist historian Gareth Stedman Jones, who coined the term "the culture of consolation" to account for what he sees as the stoical cheerfulness of much music hall comedy and vocal music, and Penelope Summerfield, who has been very important in distinguishing between different kinds of music hall, from the most disreputable to what might be called the "tamed." But no one has had much if anything to say about whistling.

Comedy, as the above-named historians agree, was at the heart of music hall. Comedy was present in patter, in mime, in song. Comic performers were often, though by no means always, well-paid, increasingly so as music hall, which began in the back or upper rooms of pubs and then achieved a new legitimacy in purpose-built theatres, spread to all cities and almost all towns throughout the kingdom. Some performers became nationally, even internationally, famous, others were local heroes. Performers and management alike took for granted a lively interchange between stage and audience. People shouted back favourite catch-phrases directed at them; they sang along with the performers.

And they whistled. Indeed, though this has rarely been noted, many of the top acts were billed as whistlers. Eugene Stratton, a visiting American performer of the end of the 19th century, was known for his rendition of "The Whistling Coon," although, as we shall see, it was not his own composition. He was one of many black-face performers who belong to a less-than glorious aspect of popular culture. In his essay, "White Skin, Black Masks: 'Nigger' Minstrelsy in Victorian England, to be found in J.S. Bratton (ed), *Music Hall: Performance & Style*, Michael Pickering writes that Stratton based his act on the cliché of the black man as "'a knock-kneed, double-jointed, humpy-plumpy smoke' whose basic pleasure consisted of whistling his happy-go-lucky way through life." "Whistling Rufus," a three-part melody with some similarity to rag music, and made belatedly popular in the 1950s by Chris Barber's Jazz Band's recording, is essentially a capering endorsement of this stereotype.

Whether Stratton inaugurated the whistling comic can't be known, but his popularity as well as talent at whistling undoubtedly had an influence on Harry Taft, one of the favourites at the Canterbury Music Hall. Taft, who was known as the "Tramp Whistler", toured the land during the early years of the 20th century, as did Albert Whelan, among whose favoured halls was the Shepherd's Bush Empire, one of the top music halls of Edwardian England. Whelan was immediately familiar to his audience from his signature tune ""Die Lustige Brüder" ("The Jolly Brothers") which he whistled as he came on stage, and again as he left it. Other popular performers of that era include Arthur Astill, "The Whistling Ploughman," and Jack Judge, who wrote "It's a Long Way to Tipperary" and, having moved from early success in Birmingham to London's main music-hall venues, developed an act which "consisted of jokes, songs, whistling, and much interaction with the audience."

That whistling on the halls didn't disappear with the Great War is evident not merely from Ronnie Ronalde's comparatively late success, but the fact that in 1940 the "Whistling Comedian" Jack Henry topped the bill at Liverpool Music Hall. But why would it? Music halls depended so largely on interchange between stage and audience that the instant memorability of songs became integral to the success of performers. In 1913, the comic singer Mark Sheridan, who was already known as the performer of the saucy "Oh, I Do Like to be Beside the Seaside," had an even greater success with "Who Were You With Last Night" ("It wasn't your sister, it wasn't your ma"), which, so a contemporary reported "is already being whistled all over the southern seaport." As Arthur Parker, the ever-hopeful peddler of sheet music in Dennis Potter's 1980's TV drama *Pennies from Heaven* says, "It's a great song, everybody's gonna be whistling it." And Lionel Bart, asked by an unctuous interviewer in the 1960s whether he wouldn't agree that he was a musical genius, modestly replied, "I'm just a bloke who can whistle a tune."

IV

Blokes — and women — whistling tunes are integral to the history and popular success of music hall. In what follows, we give details of some of the better-known performers whose names deserve to be remembered. They are by no means the only ones, but between them they provide evidence of the widespread popularity of the art they held in trust.

The already mentioned Albert Whelan was one of the first of these. Born in Melbourne, Australia, in 1875, Whelan began his career locally but moved to England at the turn of the century and was soon a top-of-the-bill performer, both in London and the provinces, as singer, dancer, pianist, and whistler. Immaculately dressed in top hat, white tie, tails and cane, he came on as a "masher" and wowed the audiences with his whistling. In 1915 he made a record of one of his most popular tunes, "The Whistling Bowery Boy," and, later, "They All Start Whistling Mary," and "Barnacle Bill the Sailor."

Billy Williams (nee Richard Isaac Bank) also came from Melbourne, where he had been born in 1878. Known on the halls as "The Man in the Velvet Suit", Williams was widely thought to be second to none as a whistler. He had great volume, accuracy, and he displayed enough variety of technique to earn himself the label "virtuoso." Unfortunately, his skills aren't especially detectable in his popular recording of "John, Go and Put Your Trousers On," and the same has to be said of a further hundred songs Williams recorded between 1907-1914, of which "When Father Papered the Parlour," was by far the best known.

Jack Judge, born a little earlier, in 1872, had no musical training. As a result, he was unable to write down "A Long Way to Tipperary", and, having whistled the tune to a friend who was able to notate it, sold the copyright in 1912 for a few pence. Nor did he ever record his most famous song. But it was made vastly popular, first by Florrie Forde, when she sang it on the Isle of Man and then the mainland in August, 1914, so Christopher Pulling reports in his history of music hall songs, *They Were Singing*. From then on, as Pulling says, troops in both World Wars adopted the song, not merely because its memorable tune combines jauntiness and nostalgia, but because the line "Goodbye Piccadilly; farewell Leicester Square," could be sung and whistled by thousands bidding farewell to their homes, even though few cared tuppence for Tipperary.

Bessie Hinton is one of the comparatively few women music hall artistes known for their ability as whistlers. At the re-opening of the Croydon Empire in 1897, she is reported by the Almanac of popular theatre, *Era,* as having "roused the gods" to emulation by her whistling of "My Bill." (Not the Wodehouse song of the same name.) Her name should be put beside that of Maud Gould, known as a "siffleuse" — presumably to lend dignity as well as glamour to her whistling, though others, too, were given the soubriquet — who featured on the bill for an early Royal Variety Command Performance, which was more than the great Marie Lloyd managed. *Her* songs and the gestures which accompanied them were considered altogether too *risqué* for their majesties. She should have stuck to whistling.

Gould, whose stage name became Madame Saberon, found a new outlet for her professional skills with the arrival of radio broadcasting. In 1924 the BBC decided to risk an outside broadcast intended to feature a nightingale and cellist. In case the nightingale declined to put in an appearance, Madame Saberon was hired as back-up. Sure enough, the nightingale had first-night nerves so Maud Gould had to deputise, although by then an inherited throat condition meant that she was forced to whistle from far back in her mouth, goodness knows how. Goodness knows what listeners made of the hoarse nightingale. Perhaps they blamed what they heard on poor reception. Radio was, after all, in its infancy and crystal sets were hardly Hi. Fi.

Most of the great whistlers began their careers before the Great War. But there were later ones and among these mention should be made of Burt Marsden, who toured the halls during the in the 20s and 30s and who in 1924 recorded "The Whistling Coster Boy." Marsden can stand for many of those who featured in the bottom half of Variety Bills during a period when music hall as a whole was at the beginning of the end.

Still at the top were Bud Flanagan and Chesney Allen, a duo of comedian-singers with more than a passing resemblance to Laurel and Hardy. Their great sing-along numbers included "Run, Rabbit, Run", and "Underneath the Arches", and typically would have a whistled passage in them. These were endlessly played on the radio, in the halls, and then on 78 rpm recordings. In a lovely moment during *Listen to Britain*, the propaganda film made by the Crown Film Unit in 1942, Flanagan and Allen, rotund Flanagan in funny hat and bow tie, the taller, lankier Allen looking as though he's almost hiding in his drab suit, stand on a rigged stage as they sing, in gentle harmony, a number clearly inspired by the success of "Underneath the Arches". "Down Sunnyside Lane", the song is called, and nothing further from the promise at which the title hints could be imagined than the grubby works canteen — *Scotch Broth, Fried Cod, Grilled Sausages,* the shaky, chalked message on a blackboard promises — where the two men loom above the shabbily-dressed workers, male and female, who, seated at their canteen tables, sway in time to the song. But then the camera, which has focussed on the comedians, reverses to show the entire audience as men and women begin to whistle in accompaniment to the entertainers' singing, and for that brief moment you feel as though the song, trite though it may be, does indeed promise a better future to be ushered in by victory over Hitler.

In post-war Britain, Flanagan and Allen, together with other comedians who made up The Crazy Gang, for years played nightly at London's Victoria Palace, their enduring popularity belying the otherwise rapid decline of music hall's status in the UK to tatty and tacky pier-end shows. The Gang Shows finished when the members died off. Elsewhere, as John Osborne's play of 1957, *The Entertainer,* testifies, music hall had already died. So, on the other side of the Atlantic, had the form of entertainment known as vaudeville, to which we must now turn.

The audience joining Flanagan and Allen in whistling
(see previous page).

V

Vaudeville — the term derives from the French Val de Vire, home
of the 18th century singer-composer Olivier Bassale — became
dominant in the USA at roughly the same period that music hall
was becoming hugely popular in the UK. From the first, whistling
seems to have been integral to vaudeville acts. One of vaudeville's
historians, Brett Page, quotes Charles K. Harris, who wrote a size-
able number of popular songs, as saying that "The way to whistling
lips is always through the heart. Reach the heart through your lyric,
and the lips will whistle the emotion via the melody. When the
heart has not been touched by the lyric the lips will prove rebel-
lious. They may indeed whistle the melody once, but it takes more
than that to make a song truly popular." There was no lack of
vaudeville performers who reached the hearts of their listeners and
who as a result enjoyed considerable success, both on stage and, in
some of the later instances, in the recording studios.

Perhaps the most famous was John Yorke Atlee. Born in
Detroit in 1842, Atlee was in demand from an early age, and by

the 1890s he was recording some of his most popular songs on wax cylinders. His reputation for virtuoso whistling guaranteed steady sales for, among others, "Our Whistling Servant Girl", and "Why Should I Keep From Whistling", presumably a rhetorical question, since, as "The Artistic Whistler" — the title by which he became known — his popularity lasted until the end of the century, at which point he began to concentrate on selling rather than making records.

George W. Johnston, born into slavery in pre-bellum Virginia a few years after Atlee, and, *pace* Stretton, known as "The Whistling Coon", was almost as popular as the older man, though his vaudeville appearances only began once he had moved to New York in the 1870s. By the time of his death, in 1914, there were many "coon" performers, virtually all of them white men who "blacked-up," but Johnston's popularity was dented less by the competition than by the deaths of three of his wives in suspicious circumstances. After the third, Johnston was tried for murder but acquitted.

Samuel Holland Rous, who took the stage name S.H. Dudley, was another popular "coon" vaudeville performer, among whose successes, on stage and early recordings, were "Whistling" (1900), "The Whistling Bowery Boy" (1904), "The Whistler and his Dog" (1905), "The Whistling Darkie" (1907), and "Whistling Johnnies" (1913). Rous also performed "Whistling Girl", in which the girl promises to marry the male singer if he whistles her a tune. Surprise, surprise. He obliges and she does him the honours.

Like music hall, vaudeville made stars of many women performers, though more of them were whistlers than their British counterparts. One of the earliest was Alice Shaw. Born in New York in 1853, she became known as "La Belle Siffleuse," under which label she toured both America and Europe, where she performed for the Russian Tsar. She was not, however, universally admired. Some complained that her whistling, though undeniably loud, was frequently out of tune. In dread anticipation of one of her tours, the London-based *Musical Times* complained that "We are threatened with the American Whistling Lady again. Is it time to put some restrictions upon free imports?"

Apparently not. At all events, Shaw was much in demand not merely as performer but as tutor, and among those she taught was Mary Scott Withers (1898-1950), "The Whistling Prima Donna", who enjoyed some success in vaudeville, as did Margaret McKee, born in the same year as Withers. McKee outlived Withers by a decade, and was admired for her rendition of the novelty number, "The Mocking Bird", which she recorded as well as always performing in her live shows. She also recorded a version of Rous's "The Whistler and his Dog".

Two other women whistlers deserve to be mentioned here. Sybil Sanderson Fagin trained as a classical singer and performed in opera before turning to vaudeville. This isn't in itself unusual. A good many singers and whistlers on both sides of the Atlantic veered between "high" art and "popular" entertainment. Count John McCormack, Sir Harry Lauder, Anne Zeigler and Webster Booth, are among those who could sing operatic arias as well as belt out popular songs, and whistlers would switch from simple melodies to the style taught by Agnes Woodward, no doubt influenced by Shaw, and known as The Californian School of Artistic Whistling. (The School actually existed.) Woodward's primer, *Whistling as an Art*, first published in 1923, went through several editions, and at a guess influenced many hopefuls drawn to the new "talkies", including singers such as Bing Crosby, who, like many popular entertainers at that time, was a skilful whistler. Many of Crosby's most famous songs were composed by the pianist Hoagy Carmichael, who whistled a passage in his recorded version of his own "Stardust", and who, as vocalist and pianist on some of the greatest jazz records ever made, with Louis Armstrong and Bix Beiderbecke, proved to have a natural affinity with the music.

The same can't quite be said of Fagin, not if her recorded work is anything to go by. But she was undoubtedly a talented whistler and among the recordings that provide evidence of her

Sybil Sanderson Fagin

skills are "The Little Whistler", (1919) and "The Nightingale and the Frog" (1920). Fagin included bird song in her repertoire, as did others, including Garcia Lucille Norman, known as "The Human Mocking Bird", who recorded, among other songs, "The

Boy and the Birds", "The Bird and the Saxophone", and "The Honeymoon Waltz", (all circa 1920), "Hawaiian Bluebird", (1926), and "Whistle Away Your Blues." (1926.) A natural jazz whistler Norman may not have been, but some at least of these wouldn't disgrace the term jazz whistling.

The other woman whistler of note is Sophie Tucker. Billed in later years as "The Last of the Red-Hot Mammas", Tucker began her stage career as "The Jewish Whistler", when she performed in vaudeville as fill-in between other acts. Quite what she whistled isn't certain, but it seems reasonable to assume Tucker's repertoire would have included jazz. And why not? Louis Armstrong was a good whistler, as were other jazzmen, including the violinist, Joe Venuti. The connections between vaudeville, "coon" music, and jazz are undeniable, though sometimes complex and fraught. They take in not merely live performance, in theatres, and dance halls, but also the growth of the record industry.

VI

Although recordings of whistlers long pre-date the Great War, the arrival of sound broadcasting gave an enormous boost to individual performers and to musicians in general, specially if they became identified with orchestras who then recorded music that was also, even perhaps usually, heard "on air." Elmo Tanner, for instance, born in Nashville in 1904, had an integral part in the popularity achieved in the 20s and 30s by the Ted Weens Orchestra. Among the numbers on which Tanner whistled were "Marvellous" (1927), "You're the Cream in my Coffee" (1928), "Heartaches" (1933 — an enormous success, so much so that Tanner's whistling created the template for much "lonesome" whistling of the following years), "Moonlight" (1939), and "Out of the Night" (1941.) After that, styles began to change and things were never the same with the Weens Orchestra, though it went on into the 1950s. Tanner himself died only in 1990.

But the 1930s was the band's and Tanner's heyday. The same may be said of Fred Lowery, probably the most successful of all whistlers during the 1930s and early 40s. Lowery, born in Texas in 1909, survived an early and terrible setback — an attack of scarlet fever left him blind from the age of two — to become at first a local celebrity, when his schoolboy skills at imitating bird song gave him his life-long nickname, "The Texas Redbird", and then go on to national celebrity. His sweet, accurate whistling, with its subtle vibrato, made his recording of "Indian Love Call" a two-million record best seller, and an LP compilation of some of his 78 rpm records, *Walking Along Kicking Leaves,* was hailed by one reviewer as the finest whistling collection ever. A modest man,. Lowery was once asked what he thought made for the attributes of a successful whistler. "Well," he said, "I think they're really the same as for any musician. He needs good musical sense — good phrasing, good timing, good improvisation instincts — and a mastering of his instrument, which in this case is his whistle."

Fred Lowery

Lowery was still touring in his sixties and seventies, and eventually died in 1994, a few years after the appearance of his autobiography, *Whistling in the Dark*.

Lowery was a master of whistling. Bob White was not. The Bob White Orchestra achieved some success on radio during the Depression years, although Mildred Bailey, who sang with her husband Red Norvo's orchestra, is on record — literally — as deriding White's lack of talent, and for once the woman with the notorious temper and acid tongue isn't being unjust. The orchestra wasn't much good, either. Bob White's music makes Guy Lombardo sound like Count Basie.

Rio Filo's band was a good deal better, to some extent because its featured singer/whistler, Muzzy Marcellino, who trained as a guitarist and violinist, and who, after leaving Filo's band formed his own, was an extremely talented performer. Marcellino whistled on the soundtrack of a number of films, most famously *The High and Mighty* (1954), the theme for which has apparently been voted by a number of radio DJs as the most whistleable of all whistled numbers. (Or do they mean the most often whistled, for the tune itself is a complex one.) Among rival contenders are "Walkin' and Whistlin' Blues" by the Four Knights, Johnnie Ray's "Just Walking in the Rain", "Big Noise from Winnetka", and "Singin' the Blues" by Guy Mitchell — the cover version by Tommy Steele was probably more popular still, in the UK. All these are easier to whistle and at different times have been heard in abundance on streets, in pubs, and, no doubt, in private places.

During the period 1930-50, a number of whistlers achieved popularity across Europe. Among them is Ilse Werner. Born in 1921 in Batavia, Werner arrived in Frankfurt aged ten but only became a German citizen in 1955. (She died half a century later.) She made over sixty recordings which feature her considerable ability as whistler, the first of them in 1934, when she both whistled and sang with Erwin Hartung on "Kunnst de Pfeifen". A fellow German, Peter Igelhoff, 1904-1978, was born in Vienna, and after spells in London and Amsterdam, moved to Berlin in 1935. He made a number of records during the war and continued to perform in later years. More worthy of note, Toots Thielemans, the Belgian musician, born in 1922, began as a jazz guitarist, then a highly skilled harmonica player, and was also a fine whistler. His harmonica playing is well represented on various studio recordings, both in Europe and America, but unfortunately very little of his whistling survives.

In this, Thielemans is less fortunate than Ronnie Ronalde. Ronalde is not to be compared to Thielemans as a musician, but as a performer he is one of the best-known whistlers in Europe of the post-war period. He was born in 1923 in London's East End, and from an impoverished early age, having discovered a talent in himself for whistling — including the imitation of bird song — he became a street busker, whistling for pennies outside pub doors. A performance of "The Bird Catcher's Song" at a school concert, led to Ronalde being taken up by Arturo Steffani. (A name reminiscent of Muntle/Mantilini in *Nicholas Nickleby*; at a guess Steffani's real name would have been Arthur Stevens.) Steffani ran a boys' choir called "The Silver Songsters", but Ronalde's ability was such that Steffani disbanded the choir and re-invented himself as Ronalde's manager and guardian/mentor.

War brought a temporary halt to Ronalde's burgeoning career, but after his demobilisation in 1945 he was advised by Steffani to study singing in London and yodelling in Switzerland. As a result, he became known as the Yodelling Whistler, and was soon recording with such success that one time he was among Columbia Records' best selling artists. His 1950 recording of "If I were a Blackbird" was for six months in the year's top twenty sellers. Among Ronalde's other popular records are "The Tritch Tratch Polka", "Bells Across the Meadow", "The Skater's Waltz", "Birdsong at Eventide", and "In a Monastery Garden". Ronalde, who made a number of world-wide tours and played Broadway, was initiated into America's North Carolina Louisburg Hall of Fame for Whistlers in 1995.

A charitable account of Ronalde's whistling style and mannerisms might note their full-blown quality. A less forgiving one would acknowledge a certain overblown element in his handling of tremolos and rubatos. Understated Ronalde's whistling isn't. In this, it has much in common with the uninhibited, let-it-all-out performances of concert-hall divas. It may also serve to rebut the hearsay notion that gays can't whistle. It isn't at all certain where or when this silliness started, but it seems to be both long-standing and widespread. At all events, in Haruki Murakami's novel, *The Wind-Up Bird*, the protagonist is at one point asked whether his poor whistling — he is an inveterate but unskilled whistler — is due to his being homosexual. Good whistling is a manly accomplishment.

The whistling of folk songs is a good deal less inclined toward coloratura and showmanship than the conventional whistling of the Halls. Perhaps because folk music is linked to wandering minstrels and Gypsy life — at least in popular imagination — whistling seems a natural partner to such music. Certainly The Corries, formerly known as The Corrie Folk Trio, make much of jaunty whistling on their recordings of "The Whistling Gypsy", "The Bonnie Lass o'Fyvie", "The White Cockade", "There are no Pubs in Kirkintillock", and "The Collier Laddie", and where they led others have followed.

Roger Whittaker also deserves mention in this context. Born in Kenya in 1936, Whitaker came to the UK in 1959, sang and whistled in pubs to earn a crust while still a student, and, as he was happy to say, acquired much of his skill and indeed repertoire from the uninhibited vocal sounds of native Africans among whom he had spent his formative years. His 1967 recording of "The Mexican Whistler", which he had himself composed, not only became a best seller, it demonstrated that he had some awareness of the whistling traditions and forms we discuss in our chapter on "Whistling as Communication", as well as a virtuosity and clarity of tone that put Ronnie Ronalde in the shade. He could have whistled "classical stuff".

VII

"Classical stuff", it may be recalled, was what Holden Caulfield's acquaintance Harris Macklin could whistle. So could Wittgenstein, once he'd recalled the notes of Mozart piano sonatas which Katherine Thomson played to him over and over again. He could also apparently whistle the entire Ninth Symphony as well as much of Beethoven's music for piano. And not to be forgotten is the whistler mentioned in *Emigrants* (based on Wittgenstein, according to Ray Monk in his biography) who could whistle arias from Bellini with such fine accuracy that, W.G. Sebald says, he recognised them years later when he actually heard the opera from which they came. In this context we should mention that Venetian errand boys and gondoliers were at one time adept at whistling operatic tunes, especially Puccini's, and that in 1889 the Belle Siffleuse herself, Alice Shaw, included in her stage act some classical pieces. It may have been she who, by example, encouraged other stage whistlers to adopt a manner — of wide vibrato and elaborate trilling — intended to bring dignity to their music, though such dignity wasn't part of the act of the transsexual whistler Baroness Lips Von Lipskill (1924-2005).

But Giuseppe Verdi was delighted when a critic complained that some of the music of *Il Trovatore*, to which he was given private access, was inferior work. "I have been writing an opera for the people," Verdi apparently told him, "not for purists and classicists like you. Now I know that in three months [the opera] will be sung, whistled and played all over Italy." He was right. Indeed, in 1894, the American Columbia Phonograph Company produced a solo whistled performance of the Anvil Chorus by John Yorke Atlee. The performance isn't up to much, it has to be said, but it at least demonstrates Verdi's sure instinct for what would please an audience beyond the coterie of opera specialists.

155

Sir Thomas Beecham is reported to have urged that "Composers should write tunes that chauffeurs and errand boys can whistle." In this he was joined by Arnold Schoenberg. "There is nothing I wish for more earnestly," Schoenberg insisted, "than that people should know my tunes and whistle them like Puccini's." Unlikely as this may seem — could even Schoenberg whistle Schoenberg? — it's at one with his optimistic hope that "one day a postman will whistle my melodies." Schoenberg loathed the music to which the Viennese bourgeoisie clung, and his move to America introduced him to the new music of jazz, by which he was thrilled.

Not surprisingly, therefore, a good deal of recorded whistling of music from the classical repertoire comes from the USA. But then the USA was at the forefront of recording music of all kinds. It is beyond the scope of this book to list these whistling recordings, but as far as recordings of classical music in the UK go, mention must be made of Edward Dolby (1906-1999), stage name Andrew Garth, a rare example in England of what was called "art whistling," and of the International Bach Society of Art Whistling, which is still active, and which performs works by, among others, Purcell, Beethoven, Mozart and Handel. The Society's name is aptly chosen, given that legend reports Bach to have been a keen whistler. So, for that matter, was Gustav Mahler, who apparently composed a whistling part for the Devil in his *Faust*, though it was never performed. And Percy Grainger, who made an arrangement of the balled "The Carman's Whistle", also composed "The Song of Democracy", intended to be whistled as an instrumental piece by a choir of boys.

More importantly, perhaps, in 1947 Benjamin Britten made a setting of John Clare's lines, "Driving Boy", as part of his Spring Symphony. The symphony, intended, in Britten's own words, to represent "the progress of Winter to Spring and the remaking of earth and life which that means", is palpably a work to sustain and encourage people living in post-war austerity Britain. In this it is very different from Vaughan Williams' almost contemporaneous 6th Symphony, black with a sense of the post-holocaust world of the 1940s. Both composers were socialists, but Britten's symphony takes heart from Clare's lines, celebrating energy, rejoicing in youthful vigour, a new start.

The driving boy beside his team
Will ore the may month beauty dream
And cock his hat and turn his eye
On flower and tree and deepening sky
And oft burst loud in fits of song
And whistles as he reels along
Cracking his whip in starts of joy
A happy dirty driving boy

A stroke of genius that Britten should have come upon lines so perfectly suited to his purpose. He also made an arrangement of the old folk song "You'll forget the Ploughboy Who Whistles Down the Lea", but where that has a plaintive nostalgia about it, the symphony's a panache and drive are to springtime. In the symphony's first movement a choir of boys whistles a melody which is echo.e.d. and magnified when Clare's lines are sung. (By Kathleen Ferrier in the opera's first performance.)

There is a poignant coda to this. Sometime after its first live performance the symphony was recorded, and while waiting in the entrance to the performance area for the engineers to do their final sound checks, one of the boys nipped to the toilet. When he emerged it was to discover that Britten had led the choir into the recording studio and the door was locked against him. End of whistling career.

VIII

Others were luckier. Even if they didn't get into the recording studios as named performers, they earned a living by whistling on film soundtracks. In the days of silent films, whistling could at least

157

be mimed, as Charlie Chaplin showed. His pursed lips and feigned cheerfulness under the threatening eyes of a policeman or a burly thug make plain that he is whistling to demonstrate an innocent unconcern. But the first important whistling in the "talkies" is chilling, sinister. Fritz Lang's *M,* released in 1931, features Peter Lorre as a psychopathic child killer at large. Before he strikes, the audience is made aware of his state of mind by his compulsive whistling of "In the Hall of the Mountain King", Greig's frantic melody mirroring Lorre's murderous compulsion. As Lorre couldn't whistle, Lang's own whistling, appropriately jerky and breathily dry, is what we hear on the soundtrack

The success of Lang's film may explain why in the following years several Hollywood films used whistling to accentuate violence and murder. Whistling — that casual, seemingly cheerful sound — provides a counterpoint, adds a *frisson,* to horror. And so in the 1932 film, *Scarface,* the gangster Tony Camonte, played with apt *froideur* by Paul Muni, whistles a theme from Donizetti's *Lucia de Lammermoor* before shooting dead his cowering victim. This plays with the commonplace assumption of an Italian taste for violence and culture going together. Bodies floating down the Arno while, above them on the Ponte Vecchio, the murderous Borgias commission paintings from some local Master. That kind of thing.

The commonplace is given an English twist when, in the 1940 film of Patrick Hamilton's play, *Gaslight,* about a socially poised, cultured middle-class man trying to make his wife believe she is insane so that she will consent to go into an asylum and he can get his hands on her money, Anton Walbrook, who plays the husband, whistles with casual, cold hearted unconcern as he sets about trying to drive the poor woman mad. Both play and film are usually dismissed or condescended to as melodrama. It seems to have occurred to remarkably few critics that Hamilton is fashioning an ingenious fable about social, class, and gender control.

Alfred Hitchcock probably did understand Hamilton's intent, and turned it to his own ends in his 1943 film, *Shadow of a Doubt.* In this example of *film noir*, Joseph Cotton plays lovable Uncle Charlie whose murderous instincts are signalled by his whistling of the famous waltz from Franz Lehar's operetta, *The Merry Widow*. Seventeen years later, in 1960, Michael Powell's *Peeping Tom* makes use of Hoagy Carmichael's "Stardust," as the murderer Mark Lewis stalks his victim, whistling, pausing, whistling, pausing, whistling .... Then, in 1971, in Kubrick's *A Clockwork Orange*, the evil-innocent Alex whistles Beethoven's "Ode to Joy" as he sets about various acts of kicking, maiming, and torturing. Finally, in this rapid survey, mention should be made of Tarantino's 2003 film *Kill Bill*, in which the same melody is whistled by the female assassin with the bee-stung lips.

Equally bee-stung lips are on show in *Niagara*, a film of 1953, in which Marilyn Monroe makes an early appearance, though it is not she but her lover who whistles the tune "Kiss", a song performed in the film by Monroe and linked to their plan to kill her husband. But now we are in the realm of sexual love, and reference has therefore to be made to that famous *double-entendre* in the Bogart/Bacall *To Have and Have Not*, of 1944. You know how to whistle, don't you, Steve? You just put your lips together and blow.[1]

Whistling in American films is customarily more innocent. It probably begins with Disney's first sound film, *Steamboat Willie*, where the only aural communication is made by Mickey, who whistles as he pilots the paddle-steamer on its treacherous way. Whistling is all-important in the same maker's *Snow White and the Seven Dwarfs*, and in 1956 reaches an unintendedly comic apotheosis in *The Man Who Knew Too Much*. Doris Day, as a mother who believes her son to be held in the prison where she is booked to perform, sings "Que Sera, Sera" to her captive audience, and as she does so the camera tracks upstairs, the song floating with it, until it reaches the ears of a young man who, having told his minder that the voice he is listening to must be his mother's, is advised "to whistle as loud as you can." Cue happy reunion.

Perhaps the most distinctive Hollywood use of whistling is to be found in the soundtracks of Westerns. One of the first of these was "The Whistling Cowboy", recorded in 1942 by Horace Heidt and his orchestra. In the following decade, such classics of the genre as *High Noon, The Proud Ones,* and *Gunfight at the O.K. Corral* made use of whistled theme-tunes, and not surprisingly whistling was therefore introduced to the Italian "spaghetti" Westerns, *Fistful of Dollars, For a Few Dollars More,* and *The Good, the Bad and the Ugly.* The scores for all these films were composed by Enio Morricone, who did his best to comply with the desire of their director, Sergio Leone, to turn away from lush, orchestral sounds — of the kind used, for example, in *The Big Country.* Leone wanted the soundtrack's music to be spare, to make use of a solo instrument which evokes solitude and expansive, remote landscapes. It may be that Leone had in mind the harmonica used so beautifully in the 1953 Western, *Shane,* but Morricone was able to call on the skills of Alessandro Alessandroni, who besides being an accomplished Italian musician and composer was an expert professional whistler. Whistling plays an important atmospheric part, then, in these spaghetti Westerns and gives them a surprisingly authentic air.

Professional whistlers, such as Merion Darlington, Muzzy Marcellino, Fred Lowery, Elmo Tanner and Roger Whittaker, earned good money by dubbing their work onto the soundtracks of Westerns as well as a wide variety of other films. They and their successors also found work in studios that made, and make, advertising film for the cinema and television and, once again, radio. Whistling has become the "key" to adverts used by Barclay's Bank in order to portray itself as an honest, down-to-earth, "blokey" organisation. DIY adverts use whistling to indicate not merely the satisfactions attendant on home improvement but, at a guess, the skills passed down from generation to generation. (Whistling may be old-fashioned, but if it was good enough for your dad, and *his* dad before him ....) Whistling is even a feature of Macdonald's advertising. We are the soul of homely goodness.

And then there are the dramas, both radio and TV, often serials which make use of whistled theme tunes. Consider, for example, the American *Dragnet* or the very English *Dixon of Dock Green*. Radio, too, can and does use whistling to create atmosphere, whether sinister or, as in the case of Tony Hancock's breathy whistling to indicate a thinking man's awareness of the pettiness of life at Number 2, The Cuttings, East Cheam, wonderfully comic.

As for the recording studios' work with pop musicians, there are more examples of whistling than might seem likely, probably because such whistling can't be replicated in live performances. Jack Smith's "I Was Kaiser Bill's Batman", a quasi-novelty pop tune of the 1970s, depended entirely on the studio for its existence; and it's to be doubted that, if and when John Lennon sang "Jealous Guy" live, he tried to replicate the whistling that threads through the recorded version, any more than Otis Redding would have whistled live his moody, lonesome, "Sitting on the Dock of the Bay." But both are memorable tunes and therefore get top marks in a test created by Tin Pan Alley. Apparently the first pressings of any new record were at one time played by studios to grey-haired cleaners and doormen in order to discover whether after one hearing they could whistle the tune. If they could, all was well. The tune had passed the old grey whistle test.[2]

IX

At the beginning of this book and at the head of this chapter mention is made of the decline of whistling in public places. It's therefore good to be able to report the recent, timely, London revival of Arthur Laurents' musical, *Anyone Can Whistle,* even if the show had a history of ill luck. (At one New York performance a member of the cast fell off stage and killed a musician in the pit orchestra.) Laurents, who in the 1950s had been black-listed as a result of the workings of the infamous House Un-American Committee, originally wrote the book of the musical in the 1960s.

161

It's about corruption and bankruptcy in small-town America, where people walk around in rags and a dodgy Professor called Hopgood claims to have to his credit five degrees, one hundred and seventeen arrests, calls himself the Pied Piper of Lunatics, and, together with Nurse Fay, has charge of the "Cookie Jar" sanatorium, the inmates of which seem saner than those on the outside..

Set against the Professor is the town's mayoress, who announces a miracle — fake water flowing from a rock — in order to bring in pilgrims and true believers and thus, she hopes, provide the town with some much-needed revenue. Naturally the scheme fails, but at the show's conclusion, Nurse Fay, who works in the sanatorium, and has hitherto been a model of control, lets rip by putting her fingers in her mouth and emitting what is described as a "shrill, piercing, ugly whistle." But it does the trick. Water starts to flow from the rock. Natural music releases natural riches.

Not surprisingly, perhaps, when the show was first performed in America, in 1964, it lasted a mere nine nights, and this despite the delights of Sondheim's musical score. The title song in particular has been recorded by a number of top-class singers, most notably Cleo Laine, though its appeal must owe more to the melody than to the lyrics.

Anyone can whistle, that's what they say — easy
Anyone can whistle, any old day — easy ....

Maybe you could show me how to let go, the singer continues, if I whistle I can lower my guard. The message is clear enough. Whistling is for free, anyone can do it, it's the music of democracy.

As a way of underpinning this optimistic note, here, finally, is a cheerful poem by Paul McLoughlin about the survival of whistling. The whistler on whom the poem is based may well be the blind whistler who was interviewed on Radio 4 early this year (2013). He comes down from Wolverhampton to London three or four times a week, and, taking a different pitch for each day, whistles for his supper. He isn't especially good, as he readily agreed in his interview, but he enjoys what he does and he is delighted that other people enjoy it, too. But it doesn't much matter whether McCloughlin's whistler is a different man. It would be good to know there was more than one whistling busker at large. Because for all that McLoughlin's whistler may not be the greatest, he's free to exercise his craft, to entertain by means of the most democratic art.

Whistling

There's a man down at the Treaty Centre,
whistling, one foot a way in front of
the other and he's rocking to and fro,
whistling, his long, white-tipped stick
stretching into a deep and lidless
tub where notes are rising.

Lately, we've been spoilt —
Peruvian pipes; a jack-in-the-box
of a singer of jaunty songs, who skips
round little children, makes them laugh;
a pensioner in a straight-backed chair
crooning into a mike to pre-recorded
tapes, Jim Reeves smoochy style;
even a blind accordionist whose playing
is an undifferentiated wash of sound.

But today none of these regulars,
just the whistler with the precinct
to himself. He takes a break, enjoys
a laughing conversation with a
punter or a passer-by. And still he rocks,
forward and back, forward and back,
his eyes enough to tell us he is blind.

But whistling? The tunnel of shops
behind him is filling with fellow
whistlers joining in — the melodies
old familiars: Bright Eyes, Somewhere
Over the Rainbow, and Alone Again,
Naturally. He isn't the greatest
whistler, the high notes clipped
as if they might be missed, but
we'll get used to him, come to accept
that we've been entertained.

Notes

[1] The American rapper, Flo Rida, in his popular song "Whistle", with accompanying video, barely rises above single *entendre* in an extended rap which openes with whistling and includes the invocation "you just put your lips together."

[2] *The Old Grey Whistle Test* became the title of a serious late-night TV programme on rock music which ran through much of the 1970s and 1980s.